D1363790

The
Omnibus
OF FUN
VOLUME 1

A Treasury of Fun
for Recreation Leaders

by Helen and Larry Eisenberg

70233

American Camping Association
5000 State Road 67 North
Martinsville, IN 46151-7902

i

ISBN # 0-87603-109-2

Cover Design and Format:
Tom Dougherty
Typeset:
Alexander and Alexander
Jennifer Cassens

DEDICATION

We dedicate *Omnibus of Fun* to the glory of God our Creator, and to those whose creative ideas have helped to make life more enjoyable for those who live in His creation. As in the original printing, we want to note some whose warm encouragement and open-handed sharing of ideas and themselves has meant to much to us:

Lynn and Katherine Rohrbough	Bert Lyle
E. O. Harbin	Mary Lib McDonald
Mary Ann and Michael Herman	A. D. Zanzig
Warren and Mary Lea Bailey	Bruce Tom
R. Harold Hipps	Wilma Mintier
Russell Ames Cook	Bob Fakkema
Ruth and Jim Norris	Wally Chappell
M. Leo Rippy Sr. and Jr.	Glenn Bannerman
Vytautas Beliajus	Howard and Lucile Tanner
Harry D. Edgren	James McGiffin
Rev. Henry Lewis	Peter Olson
Richard Chase	Ernie Yorger
Dr. Lloyd Shaw	Elizabeth Burchenal
Nina Reeves	
Warren W. Willis	

Also those whose names are in the Preface.

CONTENTS

PREFACE

When the American Camping Association, Bradford Woods, Indiana, approached us about re-publishing *The Omnibus of Fun*, we were very delighted to get the included material back in print. Here we offer ideas in organizing plans, planning parties, banquets, mealtime fun, group starters, humor, mixers, quiet and skill games which we hope you can use and enjoy.

The original 1956 book was beamed, as this one is, to:

1. The casual leader with once-in-a-while responsibilities.
2. The intermittent leader who leads more often than that.
3. Also — the recreation leader, volunteer or full time,

who needs a variety of reasonably solid, practical stuff for all kinds of situations, including camp.

Perhaps the newest field is that of fun for older adults, a growing need in church, community — and camps, retreats. We believe that most of the selected material here will be quite useful for this group, as well as inter-generational groups including all ages, and for children and youth.

Instead of footnoting, in this printing we're expressing appreciation to those whose names appeared in the original book:

Bill Jennings, Johnny Hassler, Mrs. R. H. DeHanuit, Warren W. Willis, Stell Chappell, Wilma Mintier, Northland Rec Lab, Alan Beck (in New England Mutual Life Ins. house magazine).

Roy E. Dickerson, Dr. Hugh C. Stuntz, Harry Edgren, F. L. McReynolds, J. Neal Griffith, Raymond M. Veh, Ardis Stevens, Joe Gibson, Irving Elson, David Huffines.

Rose Shill, Glenn Bannerman, Ruth Wohr Dixon, Leona Holbrook, Howard Ellis, Reynold E. Carlson, Ted Budrow, Harold W. Ewing, Richard Bowers, James McIntyre, Mrs. Martha Hammond, Edna Ritchie, Neva L. Boyd, Pauline M. Reynolds, Ivan Immel, Ralph Page, Lawrence Loy, Ruth and James Norris, Richard Chase, Scotty Burns, Peter Olson, Bill Beatty, Jane Farwell, Walter C. Cowart, Jr., Randy Thornton, Bob Tully, Frank Walkup, Bu Bush and many others whose contributions don't come to mind quickly almost a third of a century later. Please forgive us if we've left you out!

We make these acknowledgements of permissions in the Humor chapter:

Material from *Bigger and Better Boners and Boner Books*, Copyright 1952, by Viking Press, Inc., NY.

Material from *It All Started With Europa*, Richard Armour (NY: McGraw-Hill Book Co., Copyright 1955).

(continued next page)

Material from *It All Started With Columbus*, Richard Armour (NY: McGraw-Hill Book Co., Inc. Copyright 1953).

Material from *The Benchley Roundup*, Nathaniel Benchley (NY: Harper and Bros. 1954).

Material from *Cinderella Hassenpfeffer*, by Dave Morrah. (Copyright 1946-47 by Curtis Publishing Co., and 1948 by Dave Morrow. Reprinted with permission of Rinehart and Co., Inc., NY.

Material from *My Tale Is Twisted*, Col. Stoopnagle. (NY: William Morrow — M. S. Mill, Copyright 1947). With permission.

We express deep and special appreciation to James Rietmulder and his associate, Roland Burdick, for the original opportunity to do *Omnibus of Fun*, and to Lucile Lippitt, Mrs. John Van Brakle of the Association Staff, and to Mrs. J. B. Moore for typing the original edition.

Some of these wonderful friends have gone to greater joys and many have changed occupations, but their contributions continue to bring enjoyment of life. It is interesting to us that a lot that we have known personally have been such devout people in a variety of churches, communions and faiths. Social and religious are very closely related.

God bless you as you use this material to bring joy!

Sincerely,

Helen and Larry Eisenberg

Tulsa, OK
December, 1987

PART I

Planning For Fun

How To Organize Your Plans

Whether recreation takes the form of a simple gathering, like a picnic or formal party, some advance planning will help people enjoy it far more. Details that a committee responsible for the affair need to think about, devices for getting things started, things that can be done in crowded places, at big meetings, at camp, fun that develops intercultural and international appreciation, the importance of publicity, qualifications a master of ceremonies needs to have, interesting and unusual refreshments for parties and picnics—all these are discussed in this chapter.

A TESTING OUTLINE

Here is a group of questions that can be used in making the decisions about a recreational event, for use by the recreation leader or a committee planning the affair.

Why? Some groups plunge ahead to plan an event without determining why. Do you really need and want this particular happening?

Who? How many? Who should come? What age range?

What? The why determines the what. In other words, what are our real goals? Is this being held for social reasons, or to get acquainted? (If the group are already well known to each other, there is no point in playing get acquainted games.) If they are not, many get-acquainted games and mixers may be needed.

When? The time is important, particularly when considered in relation to other events taking place in the community. Is there stiff competition with something else?

Where? Often the place is settled by the headquarters of the group involved, but sometimes other facilities are needed such as social halls, skating rinks, or an outdoor spot such as a park area.

In addition, the planning committee needs to consider several other points.

1. What are the likes and dislikes of the group?
2. What activities have they participated in most recently?
3. Is there a general plan for recreation for the whole year?
4. If so, how does this event fit the plan? What should it accomplish?
5. What kind of leadership do we need to carry this through properly?

THE PLANNING COMMITTEE

There should be enough people of varied backgrounds on the planning committee to make sure that the affair is a success. Whether it is an elaborate or a simple undertaking is a factor, of course.

Sometimes a committee has been directed to plan a certain kind of party; often, however, the committee has the freedom to choose its own theme and work it out. Preparation for any particular planning session might consist of duplicating on paper or writing on the board a number of possible themes and, in addition, getting members of the group to think up some ideas themselves. The party themes suggested in this book, even if not adopted, may stimulate other ideas.

Every skillfully planned event will include most of the following elements: fellowship and release from tension; a chance to mingle, especially in small groups; opportunity for self-expression, especially in some kind of creative activity; opportunity to win or lose; creation of something beautiful, especially in music or art; rhythmic activities, if appropriate.

In other words, most parties will include the following kinds of activities:

1. Mixers, get acquainted, group starter activities.
2. Music, performed by or for the group, or both.
3. Drama and skits.
4. Active and quiet games.
5. Rhythmic activities.
6. Refreshments (something new is nice!).
7. Final opportunity for togetherness—a closing fellowship period.

Multiple Leadership. It is easier for one person to be the leader of an entire social affair. However, there are many occasions in which it is very desirable to use many different people to lead. If there is more than one leader, the order of doing things and who is to do each is important. Someone should be designated as the over-all leader or director; that person should have the freedom to adjust the program and cut out items if absolutely necessary.

FUN FOR CROWDED PLACES
(From a platform, for banquets, conventions.)

When people cannot move around freely, a recreation director must shift gears, but there are plenty of good fun possibilities. The situation can be handled in several ways:

1. Put on things all can enjoy—skits, monologs, films. The leader may become a performer and do a number of one-person stunts or he may read aloud some material (such as boners) or may do an individual performance (such as Lot's Wife). Or the leader may arrange for people to do skits and stunts. Many group starters would fit here.
2. Do things in which all can participate as a group—singing, group stunts. The group may have more fun if they can join in themselves; singing is perfect for this. Often exercisers or stretchers are good here. Such activities as having all shout their names at the same time, standing on tiptoes, or doing Football (Chapter 4).

3. Break the larger group down into duos or small groups doing some activity simultaneously. Chapter 4, Group Starters, has many kinds of material for this purpose. See also Chapter 5 on humor.

FUN AT BIG MEETINGS
(Conferences, camps, retreats, conventions.)

One of the most important things to do at the opening of a big gathering is to have several people to greet arrivals and help them find their rooms or cabins, get to the registration line, find the facilities they need, help them get a name tag, or find others to talk with.

Hello! Often a group will start from the very first with a tradition of asking all who meet each other anywhere to say "Hello". No one passes another person without speaking, and no one goes anywhere without wearing his name tag.

Signs. Many camps and conferences have signs with friendly and thoughtful greetings in the halls, over doors, and outside with wording appropriate for the age group and occasion.

At the Table. During the first two or three meals, the tables provides an excellent opportunity for getting acquainted. Leaders should be spread out at different tables, getting acquainted with participants. If breaking the ice is difficult, try conversation starters like: "What's the funniest thing that ever happened to you?" or "Have you heard a good joke lately?" This assignment can be made by announcement or by a card on each table. Let the tables discuss alternative choices in the schedule and report through a representative to the planning committee. This quickly brings people together in a small group in a natural setting and helps them become acquainted. Group Interviews (see Chapter 6) may be done at the meal if there is time.

Getting Acquainted. Right away, people are interested in four kinds of getting acquainted: with each other, with the program or schedule, with the leaders, and with the facilities. In this book are many games and mixers for all these. It is well to have leaders mix with the group during the initial period of getting acquainted. (Give leaders a different kind of name tag to distinguish them more quickly from group members.) Acquainting the group with the program and schedule can be done by talks, skits, and other presentations. Introducing the leaders with a skit is an excellent way of breaking the ice. There are games which provide excellent ways introducing the people to the facilities if they are not too widespread.

Sample Big Group Program. These activities have been used to handle up to 150 people in one large room. The group should be seated, at the start, in movable chairs.

1. Stunt. Try one of the suggestions in Chapter 4 under Fun with Noises, or Fun with Motion.
2. Handkerchief Drop. The leader drops a handkerchief; before it hits the floor, everyone is to applaud loudly (or laugh, whistle, or cheer) until it touches the floor.

3. Let's Get Acquainted. Have everyone stand and shout his name as loudly as he can. Then call "Louder, I couldn't hear you!" And again, "Louder!" Then have the group sit down.
4. Have a sing-along, preferable led by someone with experience leading songs for large groups.
5. Play marching music, have chairs moved back against the wall. Half the group moves to the center of the room and makes a circle, facing out. The other half encircles the first, facing in. As the music plays, each circle moves to its own left; when the music stops, each person does one Fancy Handshake (see Chapter 4) with one or two persons in the opposite circle. Repeat five or six times.
6. Do a simple musical mixer game for couples.
7. March the group past the refreshments.
8. Close the event with a fellowship circle with one or two closing songs well known and liked by the group.

Parties for Five or Six Hundred. Often there are occasions where large numbers of people need to get acquainted and interact. Essential in this kind of activity is advance planning and orientation of those who are to handle the people. It works well to set up a team of fifty or so leaders (the number depending on the number of guests) who work in pairs. They meet in advance of the event and learn in detail the objectives and the participating themselves in the activities which are on the schedule. (If the event is scheduled for outdoors, be sure to have an alternate site in the event of rain.)

Once people walked by serving stations where they were handed their hot dogs and picnic materials, and each was given a number. There were guides at each door to show people where the leaders with cardboard numbers on five-foot poles were located. As the participants gathered in these smaller groups, the leaders took charge and saw that the group got acquainted and completed a name tag. All who were assigned the same number ate together.

When the meal was finished, all were invited to go to the gym floor and regroup around their number. They then played two games while seated in circles. (See Pass It On or Spin the Bottle in Chapter 7.) They were then asked to sit on the floor by the stage to do group singing. Several motion songs were sung, then a group starter and skits and stunts.

FUN AT CAMP

Whether camping is done by children, youth, or adults, it is community living in the outdoors. There are several important factors involved: the people, living in groups, the camp itself, and its outdoor location.

In camp, people have an opportunity to do some things different from those they usually do at home . . . and, to do things differently. However, the camp which forgets completely to educate people for their way of life back home is not taking advantage of its full opportunity.

Generally, the objectives of camp would include helping people to enjoy and to come to love the outdoors; to find happy expression of their total selves (physical, social, mental, creative, aesthetic, spiritual) in the camp community; to gain new knowledge and new skills and therefore to grow in a wholesome, constructive way.

The recreational aspects of camp can provide a framework of expression for each camper. Through camp fun life, the camper can come to enjoy the natural setting, the pure air, the free schedule, the specialized (and perhaps spiritualized) fellowship. He can learn to rough it by sleeping in a tent or outdoors, eating plain food, participating in strenuous activities, or going on trips. Camp gives a wonderful opportunity for learning the skills of problem solving, whether these are problems in group relationships, improvising repairs to equipment, or making up new games.

Camp is a setting for forming new friendships. The wise camp staff will have present some people who are of a different cultural or racial background than are the campers. The skillful recreation leader will then see to it that there are fellowship times in which the campers can come to know these guests. Many church camps deliberately send nationals from another country to help enrich the fellowship.

Recreation at camp often takes on several groupings: (1) the entire camp, (2) cabins or groups of cabins or buildings, or (3) tribes or other groupings which may or may not follow cabin lines. Each of these will develop its own fun, much of it of an informal nature.

Cabins enjoy such fun as singing, working out skits together, writing new songs or graces for the table, sharing jokes and tricks, carrying on letter writing projects and storytelling, learning new instruments and playing them, and mastering other skills together. The organization of tribes or other groupings may be a little more formal because there are more people. They will enjoy the same things that cabins do, if the pressure of numbers does not prevent.

For the entire camp, fun ideas such as these are good:

1. Singing after meals (especially made-up songs). In one camp the leader, who has eaten first, visits the tables and helps them start songs.
2. Dramatic skits, especially improvised ones, and role playing. An effort should be made to keep such times from dropping into the old ruts of stale threadbare stunts.
3. Rainy day fun. (There might be a cabin competition for the best ideas for rainy day fun.)
4. Featuring international guests. Often they can play, sing, or tell the life in their own country, in a very captivating way.
5. Hikes, trips, trails, nature games. If you go to camp to take advantage of nature, it is a little silly to live just as if you were in the city. Special hikes to points of interest, trips of longer duration, nature trails, and nature games add to the fun. A Crazy Critter Hike, for instance, provides for having groups go out and bring back interesting nature objects, telling the whole group a fabricated story about what the name is, what the object will do. Camera hikes (perhaps developing the film at camp, if facilities are available), theme hikes such as a beeline hike (going in a straight line), book trails (reading a good book aloud after a hike into the woods) are suggestions.
6. Skill games, athletic games. If there is any objective at all for having campers take home these ideas, the plans for games may be mimeographed. Some simple games might be constructed at camp, or game boards marked on rough wood or scratched into the dirt, or mimeographed, using coke bottle caps as markers.
7. Crafts, especially including nature crafts. Here you can take advantage of the setting by using native materials, making objects useful in camp and at home. (Don't forget to practice good conservation techniques when gathering native materials.)

8. Listening to music, reading. The best camps, whatever their purpose, will see to it that some of the best music is available, to be heard, played, and sung.

9. Spiritual refreshment and recreation is a part of the program of many camps. A particular place is often set aside as an area where campers may go at will to meditate and worship in quiet. A good project might be to set up one.

10. In planning for camp activities which are enjoyable to do, don't forget work and service projects. Since recreation is more a matter of emotions than motions, a person with the spirit of fun and plan can lead campers into a worthwhile service or construction project during part of their hours and they will be happy doing it. Some camps start their season with such a work camp. Those attending usually think it's great because the fellowship of work, done in the spirit of work is great.

Big Parties for Camp. Aside from the usual opening night get-acquainted party, many camps do not plan for another large all-camp affair because they do not know how to plan one. Here are some ideas, most of which are worked out in detail in this book (see the index):

1. Circus involving the entire camp and featuring animals.
2. Mardi Gras, with parade, queens, celebrations.
3. Rodeo, with acts, side shows, making a western movie, games.
4. County Fair, featuring free acts and side shows.
5. Dramatics, stunt, talent nights.
6. Mock Track Meet, even held outdoors, perhaps near the water.
7. Football Party (or Balloon Basketball or Question Baseball).

The Staff. At camp the staff needs some recreation on its own. However, they should mix with the campers in their fun times. The planning committee should plan some affairs in which everyone can participate.

Often, the staff introduction is done with a skit, such as The Legend of Instant Postum, with each staff member wearing a sign and walking across the stage doing whatever his role requires as the narrator reads. This skit takes little preparation. Adapted or improvised skits would be effective here too. Young campers, especially, are highly interested in whether staff members will turn out to be acceptable. There is a leveling effect in skits.

The trend is for staff and campers to enjoy things together. Therefore, today's emphasis is more on cooperative, rather than competitive, activity between staff and campers. The best relationship grows in the camp in which all persons (staff and campers alike) are regarded as growing people, always on the alert to find new ways of enjoying life together.

Rainy Day at Camp. When rain comes suddenly at camp, leaders often shudder and think of the bad hours that will come from having people cooped up until the rain is over.

It is best to anticipate rain as a definite part of the total camping program, unless you're in an area where there is no summer rain. Pre-preparation will make this much easier. Note some of the suggestions which indicate saving some equipment and activities especially for rainy days. (The large group may be broken down into several small ones.)

1. Special rainy day game kit or box. This is to be brought out only when it rains.

2. Balloon games with bright colors to drive the gray away. (See the chapter on Quiet Games.)
3. Puzzles, saved especially for rainy days.
4. Some simple, quick crafts especially for rainy times.
5. Active indoor games, relays, and contests.
6. Playing mystery or send 'em out of the room games.
7. Have a Mock Track Meet (see the chapter on Quiet Games).
8. Bring out table games.
9. Have a quiz show, one group versus another.
10. Use one of the large group party ideas, like quickie Circus or Football Party, for life and action (materials having been gathered in advance).
11. Save your birthday celebrations until rainy days and then put on a big one. (Everybody will want it to rain then!)
12. Teach some new games.
13. Play Ping-Pong Football, Balloon Basketball. (Several games could be going at the same time if you have several ping-pong tables and a number of large balloons.
14. Do some good group singing, learn new lively songs. Encourage campers to make up songs.
15. Play Camouflage (see the chapter on Quiet Games.)
16. Have an indoor picnic for a meal, using all imagination possible (even with a few cut-out ants!).
17. Have "cook-in" instead of a "cook-out", furnishing campers with precooked weiners to put on real or imaginary sticks. Have them toast marshmallows. Set the atmosphere for imagination.
18. Use a radio or TV if they are around. If campers would like such a program, tune in on a ball game.
19. Storytelling, reading. Some of the humorous material in this book and others might be read or told. Have a continued story going around a circle of campers (making sure the circle is not too big).
20. Make up stunts and put them on. Allow campers to take off leaders or counselors.
21. Play charades.
22. Have string horse race or turtle race (see the chapter on Quiet Games).
23. Make paper sack puppets and put on a puppet show. Or have a show by some puppeteers who are in camp, presented for the enjoyment of all.
24. Show a movie or slides, especially with outdoor scenes and lovely color to cheer up spirits.
25. Have a Christmas celebration. Campers might make gifts, exchange them. Sing carols.

INTERCULTURAL FUN

For a thing to be genuinely intercultural, there needs to be genuine interest first, interest in persons. If people are genuinely concerned, they will develop friendships with those of another cultural group. This may involve setting persons of Indian, Chinese, and Negro groups to seek out friendly white groups; Spanish American or Italian or Polish groups to select English-speaking groups as well as the reverse. The approach should be genuine and open. The self-contained group misses the richness of fellowship by not enjoying that of others different from themselves.

One of the best ways to interchange is to enjoy food together. Many camps have an entire evening devoted to the eating of foods, sharing of cultural gems of a particular group. If that group customarily sits on the floor to eat, so do the campers. If a person of the nationality group is present, there may be questions and answers. "Why do Japanese sit on the floor?" "What is the basis of the custom?" The questions should be asked with a desire to understand.

Intercultural meetings will not necessarily make one love everybody in the group. Genuine love is preceded by understanding and appreciation; it involves coming to understand and appreciate people and people's customs without necessarily adopting those customs. Real appreciation takes time.

In learning songs, stories, dances from other cultural groups, it is more important to be sincere than to be correct. A Lithuanian appreciates your effort when you try to learn his language even though your pronunciation and style are off. A genuine festival will bring an interchange of ideas. It will be developed in the atmosphere of appreciation for each other—the treasures of nationality and cultural groups. Real intercultural effort may also involve asking people from one culture to perform a dance or sing in the language of another.

Many groups will have to have their intercultural fun second-hand. By using records and books and piano music and their best knowledge, they will enjoy these cultural gems. If so, try to explain the background for whatever is used.

It is not necessary to be a folk lore student to do a creditable job on a folk festival. Groups can easily work up some material, do their best on native costumes, and present their wares. Folk singing and general games add to the program.

It is always interesting to learn a few words in another language, such as how to say "hello", "how are you?", or "goodbye". A person who speaks another language may get quick attention by teaching such short phrases as these.

FESTIVALS
(Regional, International—small, large)

Regional festivals such as strawberry festivals, and international folk festivals are becoming increasingly popular in community and city for large group fun. Some of these are held indoors, some outdoors; some are annual, some are even triennial. Others may be small ones sponsored by a troop, school or church group.

It is good to have the purpose clear before going further. What is the festival to do? Acquaint those who take part and those who attend with the past history of the area? Acquaint people far around with the commercial products of the area, such as strawberries, oranges, or tulips? Point up history? Help to interpret America as a land of many threads of cultural background? All are possible. Which is the group trying to accomplish?

Historical Festival. If this is decided upon, a writer should be engaged to create a script, bringing in a number of scenes of history, and using many of the folk of the community. Old settlers should be included, descendants of early families. Libraries and records should be checked. This kind of production should occupy several months in preparation and call for large local participation. It should last for several days.

Flower or Fruit Festival. Usually such things as crowning a queen, having a parade with floats, having a big celebration in which demonstrations of singing and dancing take place are the order of the day. Sometimes athletic contests are held in connection with the festival. The particular flower or fruit of the region is the keynote.

International Festival Ideas. In celebration of United Nations Week or some other organizing time sponsored by school, church, or clubs, many groups have international festivals. In them are featured songs, stories, games, poetry, dances, and crafts from around the world. Such affairs will feature these items:

1. A colorful Parade of Nations, decorating floats in keeping with the theme.
2. Foods of the Nations. Foods of different countries could be served through a window or door in a housefront designed like a typical one of that country. Foods might also be served at a banquet or as refreshments.
3. Crafts Around the World. Displays can be set up around the edge of a large social hall and those attending are welcome to visit the booths and ask questions.
4. Play Around the World. This could be featured as part of the program itself or could be in booths or displays with figures and dolls representing the manner of play of the children and adults of different countries.
5. Courtship Around the World. A party involving international students showing, in skit form, courtship as it is customarily done in different parts of the world.
6. Films from Around the World. Film showings, during or preceding the festival, help to give atmosphere and to bring understanding of how the people in another part of the world live, work, play and worship.
7. Music Around the World. With recordings, solo singers, or group singing, this theme may be carried out.
8. Dancing Around the World. If appropriate, demonstrations and group participation give a picture of how people enjoy this form of recreation.

A Festival Program. Since the age, number, and condition of participation infestivals varies greatly, it is difficult to say just what should be done. Here is a pattern which might be modified to your situation.

I. The Pre-Program Features

International crafts, foods, dolls, products are displayed. Films shown. Music, live or recorded, played as background. Games shown.

II. The Festival.

1. Parade of Nations. People carrying flags of many countries. Place them in positions of honor on stage or in front of the group. Here some groups may plan in invocation.
2. Processional of festival folk.
3. Demonstrations and performances by folk singers, dancers, poets, and craftspersons.
4. Group singing by all.

5. More demonstrations.
6. Participation by all in simple folk activities, such as singing games, folk games, with or without records.
7. The whole group seated together again for a story, singing, and closing. (Religious groups may want to close with a prayer of brotherhood and benediction.)

Some Suggestions and Pointers for Folk Festivals

Out of the experience of many folk festivals has grown certain suggestions which will aid those who are trying a festival for the first time:

1. Practice what is done so that it will be well done. However, perfection is not so much the object as spontaneous fun. Well-covered-up mistakes may add more flavor to the affair than perfection. (One girl lost her skirt in the middle of a performance. She reached, picked it up unabashed, and held it in place until time to leave. She got thunderous applause!)
2. The keys to success are color, action, and change of pace. There should be a good climax at the end. If the ending is on the stage, something involving every participant is good.
3. Keep the tempo moving. This does not mean that it won't slow down during a quiet solo performance. However, after the performance, have something planned to pick up speed again.
4. Capitalize on the experience of your group in foreign lands. This will help to keep them from seeming foreign.
5. Look for natural places to present such affairs. A denominational youth group uses a quadrangle on a college campus, setting up booths and doing folk games on the green. One of the buildings has stairs leading to a second floor entrance and the landing makes an ideal spot for the leader and the public address system.
6. Get a theme, but don't let it dominate completely. If there are worthwhile features that do not fit the theme, they may still be used.
7. Pre-preparation of groups is good; it creates anticipation and the practice improves the final performance.
8. Attend a smoothly operating festival to get ideas; even the large ones will provide ideas which others can use.
9. Provide some participation for everyone as part of the festival. Keep the part very simple.
10. If the festival is held outdoors, and there is a place to go indoors, plan what each member of the committee is responsible for if it rains. In this manner, the festival can change location and equipment can be taken care of without losing time or without damage.
11. Any festival will benefit from the presence of people from other countries. In a small one, give every person who desires it the opportunity of talking with the performers with different backgrounds.
12. Unusual musical instruments, like the sitar from India or the mbira from Africa, are particularly interesting for demonstrations.
13. Films from these countries may be shown in advance at the meeting of the group prior to the festival. Learning their songs may add interest too.

14. If stories are used, be sure to get the people seated reasonably close together and have the storyteller in a position where all may see and hear. Even recorded stories may be received well under these circumstances. The master of ceremonies should see to it that there is quiet, even if it is necessary to interrupt the storyteller and insist upon quiet.

15. The embassies of some countries will furnish information and pictures. Some airlines have travel posters for decorations.

16. Specialists in folklore should be used, especially for leading or directing. These do not need to be professionals, but they do need to be proficient.

17. Be sure to have authentic foods of the countries if at all possible. Arrange with people from various countries to prepare food or at least supervise the preparation so that it will have that special flavor.

PUBLICITY FOR RECREATIONAL EVENTS

Telling everyone about a party or other recreational event is as important as planning a good one! The sky is the limit when it comes to using imagination for publicizing. Some suggestions are included here; one of the chief ones is to modify, change, adapt, brainstorm so that your group will come up with creative publicity to intrigue people and make them come to whatever it is you're putting on—party, festival, circus, supper, money raising affair, athletic contest.

Mailings. Post cards, letters, booklets, flyers sent through the mail will attract some attention, especially if sent in more than one mailing. A post card is a good advertising medium because you almost have to read it, even as you are throwing it away. Handwritten mailings, personalized, are more effective than printed or mimeographed ones; even a note in the margin helps to personalize it. Cut out unusual shapes to mail in the invitations: a lively witch, a grinning pumpkin, a cheerful heart, a lively Father Time, for the rhyming invitation that you will send. Some groups have members address envelopes to themselves. Then, when the invitation comes through the mail, they read it because the envelope is in their own handwriting. Besides paper, such material as dried ears of corn, bolts and nuts tied with string, or a sucker, can be mailed. (The first might be an invitation to an African safari; the second could state, ''Don't think we're nuts . . .'', and the third, ''Don't be a sucker and stay away.'')

Telephone. This is a fine method because it is personal. If each person on the telephone committee will call a small number of people, the experience can continue as a personal one. (''Each one call one'' might be instituted. I call you, and give you the name of another person to call, and the name of a person for that person to call.) The mystery element might be brought into telephoning, not telling who is calling, or assuming some famous or majestic name.

Bulletins, Bulletin Boards, Announcements. Most groups have bulletin boards where announcements and posters can be placed. (Make it mysterious—use several changes of announcements.) They can also be made in meetings, bulletins and newspapers. In meetings, it is much better to have a skit or stunt to present the idea than a mere speech. Have people walk through meeting places with signs (where appropriate) to advertise the coming event. Get those who have tickets to wear badges. (Perhaps the ticket itself is a badge.)

Signs on Cars, Drinking Fountains, Waste Baskets, Hanging from Ceiling. Go all out; let them see word of the coming event everywhere they turn. People wearing tags will publicize it too.

Discs, Tapes. Use them to broadcast the news; if not too expensive, mail out recorded discs as advertisers.

Poster Contest. This would stimulate interest, and the best posters (and the worst ones too) could be displayed. Often stores will cooperate.

Radio, Television. Sometimes local stations will give publicity to coming affairs. If you use a skit, rehearse it, make it punchy, and keep it brief.

"Commando." Have little groups in cars or on bicycles who are carrying announcements. They deliver them quickly, go on to the next place. Best done two by two.

Singing Commercials. Performed at meetings, over the radio. A contest to see who can compose the best.

Clown with Signs. He strolls around at meetings, or stands on a street corner; he may give out handbills, too.

Election of King and Queen. Names not revealed until the affair begins.

Pictures, Slides. Display pictures taken at the last year's affair. Take a set of colored slides for publicizing next year's affair.

Quick Sign Making. Tempera and show card colors are fine for signs, but very quick and attractive ones can be made from colored chalk on colored construction paper (large sheets). For quick signs, use liquid shoe polish brushed on with the dauber.

THE MASTER OF CEREMONIES
(See also The Toastmaster, in the chapter on Planning Banquets, Mealtime Fun)

The Master of Ceremonies is the director of festivities. He or she has something of the same functions as the Toastmaster, but may have broader responsibility. Very likely the MC has been with the planning committee and has helped line up the program, acts, presentations, and speakers. He is the one who keeps things moving, sees to it that program items are ready, that the performers are introduced, and that the program closes on time. The good Master of Ceremonies, like the Toastmaster, will keep some humorous material at his disposal, either in his head or on cards or in a notebook. When appropriate, he brings out a pointed bit of humor.

An MC will also find it helpful to make out a timing list for the program and keep it handy on a small index card. He should plan in advance how much time to allow for each item and urge the performers to stay within their time allotment.

In making presentations of persons, speakers or acts, the MC should say sincere, sensible things, perhaps with just a little flourish. Over elaborate statements and introductions may leave the audience feeling as people do at a county fair when they have eaten cotton candy.

Have some expander items in the program which could be eliminated, if timing is too long. Most programs run a third longer than anticipated—some twice as long. If you have some things which could be cut out, you can still end on time. Business meetings are particularly bad about taking more time than anticipated. If an item has to be cut from the program, you may want to apologize for its omission and express your appreciation for the graciousness of the performer who has been superceded.

Sometimes a Master of Ceremonies is supposed to play role, such as the Ringmaster, or President of a college. You may need to spend some time getting a proper costume; shops rent them for a nominal amount. At least improvise to keep within the theme idea. But, do not call undue attention to yourself; you are the chairman, not the star performer.

Plan to honor those who deserve it; there is nothing more delightful to those who have worked long and hard than to have their work recognized. Depending on the occasion, have them stand for applause, for a lively song dedicated to them, perhaps for a gift. "Happy Birthday" is music in the ears of the most sophisticated, especially if it is a surprise cake with candles.

Be kind to participants, especially if they are timid. The attitude of the audience toward the whole experience will be resting heavily on your relationship with your performers, as well as with them.

Plan for more humorous material and group singing than you will need, but be ready to condense.It is always good to have a number of possible items grouped in categories, if you yourself are to lead.

If a good many are to participate have an understood signal for finishing. One group used a green, amber, and red light in view of the person speaking but not the audience. When the amber came on, he had two more minutes; on the red, he was to stop.

Building a Program. Change of pace, variety, balance, and audience participation are important in programming. For this reason, it is good for you as MC to begin with some group group starters (see the chapter by that name), group singing, and the like. This warms up the audience and lets them get some of the fun of performing. Start with some of the best items, presentations, or acts. This is the technique of professionals. Use an interest catcher at the start.

Do the same at the end, closing with a climactic number on a climactic note. This means saving one of your best singers for the closing feature, having a song or two of rousing group singing, or getting the entire company of performers to do something.

Many masters of ceremonies like to end the program with a thought for the day. Groups with religious motivation may use spirituals, hymns, prayer, or sing "The Lord's Prayer" in unison as a closing. There should be a clean, clear dismissal of some sort.

The best master of ceremonies learns to play the group by ear, sensing when they are restless (giving a breather, a stretcher, or opening windows), noting when they are happy and contented, and doing as nearly as he can what they want done.

Credit to those who have made the meeting possible is a must, of course, including thanks for the use of facilities, gratitude to planning committees, and the kitchen crew, especially when they are all volunteer labor.

ENDINGS FOR PROGRAMS

At the end of a recreation program, many groups want a quiet time of fellowship, thoughtfulness, consciousness of harmony and perhaps prayer. At least, a climax is desirable.

The ending is used purposely to draw people back into a sense of togetherness after refreshments. Here are some of the things that have been used successfully.

Fellowship Circles. Since the circle formation is used so much, it is appropriate to close that way. In the circle you can see everyone, and holding hands around the circle makes for a nice ending. Singing takes place, often leading from a lively song to a quiet one, to a hymn or spiritual and closing prayer.

Seated, Quiet Singing. An appropriate setting for this is outdoors around the campfire, on the steps of a building, or in the vesper kind of beauty spot.

Spiral Circle. A more formal kind of ending is sometimes used in which all are given candles to carry and they start in a circle, slowly drawing into a spiral, with song and words in that formation.

Closing with "The Lord's Prayer". Many groups close regularly by singing together Malotte's "The Lord's Prayer." It is very impressive in an international gathering to have the prayer spoken, each in his own tongue.

Story Reading or Telling. Starting with fun material, the group may sit in some natural rallying center for story reading or telling. Some Scripture passages are especially enjoyed in an outdoor setting like this.

Galilean Service. If near the water, some groups like to use that setting, having their performers come up in boats. Be sure that the boats are seaworthy. and that no one rocks or tips them.

Echo Singing. At a natural beauty spot in a summer conference setting, it was discovered that one group, going to the point, could be heard across the water half a mile away by another group. The ending much enjoyed there, now, is to cross the lake and sing back and forth.

Start A Song. Sitting in near darkness, perhaps around a fire, anyone in the group is invited to start a song. Fun songs, love songs, folk songs, or spirituals can be used. A designated person may close by announcing the final song.

What Have You Enjoyed Today? Often that question will be asked as the group is quiet and relaxed. The answer will be appreciated by the hard working leadership. The mood for the closing is set somewhat by the remarks. This might bring some suggestions about the schedule or procedure, before the final closing.

A Presentation and Singing. At the end of the day after a fun period, there is a nice lull in which a presentation can be made. Once a gift of an autoharp was given and the receiver played the autoharp to accompany a song or two before the closing.

Indoor Campfire. As well as the crepe paper over the light kind, several candles grouped together in a safe manner can give the effect of a fire, without the heat of a fire.

Thought for the Night. A two-minute talk, centered around a single thought of uplift will send people away with a sense of completion.

Closing Centering around a Person from Another Country or Racial Group. If this person conducts singing, it deepens the fellowship to have him lead.

Worship Service with a Theme. Such a service may be brief but very effective. A tendency in many groups is to overdo it, using too much material for people who are tired and want to get to the refreshments or home. Be single minded and brief.

Planning Parties

2

Novelty and the surprise element are half the fun of a party. The clever party planner thinks up fresh ways of inviting guests and new approaches to old games as well as new ones. In this chapter is a list of nearly 120 intriguing ideas which may spur the reader to concoct still more original ones around which to build a party. Here too we find some 32 suggestions for making brief social periods exciting. Then full details are given for parties on New Year's Day, Valentine's Day, Washington's Birthday, April Fool's Day, Halloween, and Christmas, as well as for a Space Party, a Circus, a Football Party, and a One World Party.

IDEA STARTERS

Clock Watchers. Employees' party.

Lonesome Party. Get together and write to those in group who are away, also to anybody else who might be lonely.

Kaffee Klatsch. Coffee-and-talk affair, perhaps with a few acts, jokes.

Storytellers. Liar's Convention.

Movie Party. Go to one, return to group headquarters for refreshments and informal discussion of movie.

Walking Rehearsal. Play reading for small group.

Window Shopping Party. Give two or more groups one hour to go window shopping, return to meeting place to report adventures. Have quiz.

Round Trip. Short excursion on train or bus.

Prodigal Son. Someone who has been away returns.

Toy Patch. Repair toys before Christmas.

Sculptors. Small party for those interested in trying their hands with a little clay. Or, it might be work party to carve old plaster off prior to removing partition.

Better Half. You bring yours, couple games planned.

Gourmets. Something very unusual to eat, with table games. (Or something very low-brow such as hot dogs.)

Park Party. Go to park for fun, eat picnic supper together.

Bible Party. Games come from Bible entirely. Play might be presented.

Back at the Ranch Party. Western idea, garb, games, contests, food.

Psychiatrists' Convention. You fill in blanks.

Cabinet Makers. Build some cabinets needed in organization.

Dessert. Eat at home, but come for dessert, conversation, and games.

Mother Goose. Games come from that source.

Mere Maid's Party. For girls.

Neptune Party. Swimming party.

Garden Party. Home party idea.

Juke Box. Record party.

Photography. Make, develop pictures.

Nationality. Invite others. Do things from their lore. Swedes, Czechs, Italian, Chinese, Mexican, or whoever is in your community.

Let's Learn It. Anything.

Whittling. Learn to whittle, wood-carve.

Rod and Reel. Fishing trip.

Quiz. Feature quizzes, listen to TV programs.

River Boat. Go out on one.

Coffee Break. Enliven them with themes, posted. Jokes—embarrassing moments—acts.

Autoharp. Learn to play it.

Continued. Break party up in more than one section —part on one day, part on another.

Rodeo. Shoot the works. Acts, color.

Barnyard Frolic. Animal show, animal games.

Smorgasbord. Put on one.

Come As You Are. When telephoned, come as you were dressed.

Sloppy Joe. Dress-down party.

Knights of the Road. Tramp party.

Radio TV. Put on acts or go to studio.

Ocean Crossing. Ship party.

No School Today. For kids.

Table Games Party. Play 'em.

Old Mill. Find one, go to it, have storytelling, days of yore. Outdoor games.

Fireman's Shindig. Games, rescues, and the like.

Tourists. For them, if appropriate.

Income Tax. They get together for mutual help.

Refrigerator. Raid it, freeze stuff.

Talent Night. Roundup of talent. Talent scouts.

Hobby Lobby. Hobby show, lobbying for hobbies.

Alpine Party. Climb real mountain.

Sightseeing for Fun. Group, family, or person could go; or this could be imaginary trip, or one with kodachrome slides, movie series, or lecturer.

Coffee Party. Serve coffee and dessert, play table games, do simple crafts, converse.

Trail Party. Drop confetti to mark trail. At end of trail have cookout, picnic meal, roast weiners, or storytellers convention, read aloud outdoors.

Street Fair. Another organizing idea like County Fair.

Indoor Picnic. All features of outdoor one, but held indoors, even in living room. Or Moonlight Picnic in yard, with Japanese lanterns for light.

FBI Roundup. Meet at regular place, go out and round up all erring members you can find, and have party. Send two agents to call on each one.

Fun-O-Rama. High-sounding name for carnival type of social affair.

Suppressed Desire Party. Come dressed appropriately for your suppressed desire (but wear something). Act out suppressed desires.

Gay 90's Party. Celebrating all music, games, and customs of Gay 90's, even down to box social.

Flat Earth Party. Using this theme (instead of round the world) have things in four corners of room. Use square dances. Refreshments could be flat.

Capsule Party. Fortunes, forfeits, acting out suggestions are contained in capsules. The party itself may be shortie. Capsule relay: run up to chair, take capsule with water, run back and touch off next person in line.

TABLOID SOCIALS
(Social periods of 20-60 minutes for youth and adults)

There are more occasions in most groups for using a short social period of 20 minutes to an hour than for the 2½- to 3-hour party. Therefore, some suggestions are included for these fun periods such as those for men's and women's clubs, for after-meetings, including youth groups on Sunday nights, brief periods at school, part of a family night program, sometimes at home, dorm parties, student center.

The principle of this kind of social period is that it moves fairly fast in developing a sense of group spirit. Often the group is a small one. Use mixers if needed. If the group has been together, they may not be needed. Group singing is one of the most valuable tools for this kind of social time. The next best ally is probably the simple chair game, and equipment games of the bean-bag-shuffleboard-ping-pong variety. Table games are also good, as is record listening.

Helps for most of these ideas below are found in this book.

1. Progressive Party, from house to house. This is mostly for exercise if time is limited.
2. Walk or ride to someone's home (or back yard) for fun with equipment games, refreshments.
3. Singing evening, with folk-song book, spiritual collection, hymnal. Just singing for fun.
4. Creative writing, or use of other creative materials on tables, such as paints, clay, finger paints. Relax and see what you can do.
5. Puppet show. Either present one with puppets already made or else make some paper-sack puppets and put on brief show (divided into two or more groups).
6. Balloon Basketball Game. (See Chapter 7) This may occupy most part of 20 minutes with fun. Build toward it a little, and have sides. Use frequent substitutions so that, if there are not too many people, everyone plays.
7. Quickie version of Football Party. It can be done in 45 minutes with enjoyment.
8. Charades. This is favorite of informal groups.
9. Skits, stunts. Pre-prepared, or divide up and let each of several groups present stunts.

10. Situation drama. Same idea, but give each group a situation to be worked out and presented.
11. Remembering shut-ins. Go singing to them, caroling in season, take along tape of group performance or of Sunday's sermon, or plan some other group activity for their enjoyment. Visit briefly and leave.
12. Story reading, storytelling. For brief, easygoing time have good storyteller, or someone who can read humorous material to do just that. Fireplace is ideal.
13. Birthday parties. They could be celebrated briefly and special surprises presented.
14. Letter writing. Get together around tables, eat popcorn or potato chips or apples, write letters to absent members of group, send cards to those who should receive them. Even make some original cards.
15. Equipment, table games evening. Around small tables, have number of games available of checkers, chess, Chinese checkers, Scrabble variety. Refreshments, too, of course.
16. Big Trip. Someone who has been on trip shows his kodachromes to appreciative audience. Several could share vacation pictures in one sitting in this way. Could be called "The Picture Show." If there are several new babies in couples' group, this might be way of getting all this off at same time.
17. Travel movies or slides, professionally made and genuinely entertaining.
18. Penny Push. (See Chapter 7.)
19. Window shopping. For group not too large, in town, this can be relaxed fun. Go somewhere for refreshments.
20. Treasure Hunt. Over previously laid out course (indoors or outdoors) crowd, in small groups, looks for hidden treasure. This would not have so many clues as full-fledged 2-3 hour treasure hunt.
21. Concert. Either at group meeting place or in home, listen to some records. They could be long-hair, short-hair, comic records. Television or radio program might be sandwiched in.
22. Bull session. Get together over refreshments around small tables for gab fest. There might be topic to start, but conversation quickly wanders.
23. Talent show. This would be briefer than full-fledged one. Several numbers could be presented now, and several this same time next month.
24. Campfire and fun. Fun consists of singing, informal stunts, joke telling, humorous material of other kinds, storytelling, dozing comfortably. Basket of apples passed about constitutes refreshments, perhaps. Campfires or hearth fires are good rallying centers.
25. Picnic, weiner roast. That would be all you'd have time for—no program.
26. Mock Track Meet. This actually isn't very wild (see Chapter 7). It could be great fun.
27. Kaffee Klatsch. This is just another European name for coffee time, which could include anything for program or nothing. Perhaps table stunts, tricks with matches, puzzles, could be used.
28. Prodigal Son Celebration. Member of group is back in town. You honor him with brief party.
29. Dessert Party. Someone invites group over home for dessert and fun.
30. White Elephant Party. Bring your white elephants and trade or auction them off. How did you get 'em in first place?

31. Chili Party (or any other food). If group is not too large, let them help prepare, or at least finish preparation. This could include hamburger fry, weiner roast or boil. One church group takes great delight in "potato fry." They wash, peel, fry and eat potatoes, night after night.

32. Most of theme party ideas could be reduced to "shortie party": New Year's, Valentine's, George Washington's Birthday, Fourth of July, St. Patrick's Day, Labor Day, Thanksgiving, Hallowe'en, Christmas. Certainly tables where refreshments are served can be fittingly decorated. Group could be asked to make hats of suitable style and wear them for atmosphere. One or two equipment games could be used, such as "horse racing game" adapted to theme. (Turkey race, cat race, and the like.)

VALENTINE PARTY
(Ages 9 and over)

Here are some possible titles: Land of Heart's Desire, Festival of Hearts, Cupid's Excursion, Hearty Party.

As in any party, decorations are important. Decorations could include hearts, red and white crepe paper streamers, comic valentines on the walls, aching, bleeding, broken hearts all over the place. Cupids, lacy decorations are appropriate.

Name tags are often heart-shaped, though they may use the comic valentine idea also. One party used a lei (Hawaiian style) of small hearts, placed around the necks of the guests.

Some organizations have the girls put on the party and bear the expense. Often it is better not to have people come in couples nor to plan all the games that way, since the number of guests coming will be uneven. Those without partners feel left out unless provision for them is made. Use musical and folk games in trios, those that allow stealing partners and the like.

For early comers, skill games such as Heart Darts (throwing darts at a heart-shaped cardboard target), Make an Original Valentine (from doilies, construction paper, scissors, paste, magazines, crayons, and other colors), or trying to flip a red-painted ping-pong ball from a coke bottle (which is dressed in Valentine garb).

Musical games are appropriate to start off with: a Hearty March (Grand March), a Hearty-Cake Polka (Patty-Cake), Cupid's Clap (The Clap Marlene), "A Toast to Cupid Who Is Brave and True." (By adapting slightly and changing titles, many folk and musical games would be appropriate.)

For group singing, use the heart songs, like "I Love You Truly," "Let Me Call You Sweetheart," "Tell Me Why," "Springtime in the Rockies," "Four-Leaf Clover," "Carolina Moon," "Harvest Moon." (Since most of these are somewhat sentimental, singing is usually used late in such a party.)

For getting partners, cut hearts in two, using unusual cuts that must be matched. Those whose hearts do match are partners.

Games for Valentine Party. Spin the Bottle becomes a spinning arrow, to determine in the seated circle (or circles in groups of over thirty) who has the biggest feet, broadest smile, loudest tie, best cupid's bow lips, brightest socks, heartiest laugh, greatest heart-breaker, who will marry first.

Whose Heart Did He Win? When leader calls out the name of one member of a famous couple, see who can supply the other name.

1. Adam	—Eve	12. Saul	—Ahinoam
2. Esau	—Judith	13. Jacob	—Rachel
3. Abraham	—Sarah	14. Joseph	—Mary
4. Ahasuerus	—Esther or Vashti	15. Boaz	—Ruth
5. Elimelech	—Naomi	16. Agrippa	—Bernice
6. Ananias	—Sapphira	17. Zacharias	—Elizabeth
7. Isaac	—Rebekah	18. Samson	—Delilah
8. Ahab	—Jezebel	19. Joseph	—Asenath
9. Moses	—Zipporah	20. Aquila	—Priscilla
10. Elkanah	—Hannah	21. David	—Michal and
11. Lamech	—Adah		Abigail

Clap Out Rythm (of a love song). Divide into groups, each group claps out the rhythm of a love song for the others to guess.

Play games involving forfeits. (See Forfeits in Chapter 7, for ideas.) "Heavy, Heavy Hangs Over Thy Head" may be over the King or Queen of Hearts' Head.

In small groups or in couples, using magazines, have them clip and paste to compose love letters to be read. Check your favorite game book for some which can be adapted to the theme by changing the names or references. Refreshments could include heart-shaped cakes or cookies, heart-centered ice cream, "Love Potion" of red fruit juice and the like. Singing sentimental love songs makes for a good conclusion.

CHEERY CHERRY PARTY
(Ages 9 and over)

Here are some suggestions for a Washington's Birthday party that may be new to your group.

Group Starter. Give each guest a number. Divide into five teams. General Washington will ask each team to:

1. Find as many words as possible from George Washington.
2. Get names of all persons present with black hair, blue ties (or whatever is decided upon).
3. Get names of all people starting with M (for Martha) whether first or last name.
4. Find out who has birthdays during month of February.
5. Present skit from Washington's life using whatever costumes and scenery are available on the spur of the moment.

Chopping Down the Cherry Tree. Tell a story, the group standing in a circle. When the word, "hatchet", is mentioned, each must drop to one knee. The last one to do so becomes It.

Shaking the Cherry Tree. While one person (cherry tree) is blindfolded, others recite:

Oh, here's a tree of cherries ripe,
A tree both green and tall.
We'll shake it now with all our might
Until the cherries fall.

One person shakes tree gently; then, the tree tries to guess who shook him or her.

Reciting the Declaration of Independence. Box of candy to anybody who can do it!

Truth or Consequences. Ask several people (by number) to come forward, and ask them questions to which they must tell truth or pay consequences (see Forfeits and Consequences, Chapter 7).

Musical Games. Patriotic names or Early American names can be given to them. Virginia Reel or Circle Virginia Reel would be appropriate.

REFRESHMENTS: Virginia ham sandwiches, United States Punch (cherry and pineapple juice, in blue cups). Drums can be made by baking cake in round cans, cutting slices 2 inches thick, cover with icing, decorate with red, white, and blue. Remove centers, fill with cherry ice cream.

KING APRIL'S BIRTHDAY
(An April Fool Party for older children, youth, adults)

Decorations could be in keeping with April—showers. (This would call for umbrellas, flowers. Crazy decorations would be appropriate. King April has throne.)

Each person is to bring April Fool surprise, like joy buzzer, end of thread through coat (running to spool of thread in pocket of wearer), drinking glass that leaks, hot chewing gum from novelty store.

Around room will be April Fool traps of various kinds, like object wired with low volt electricity. Over some perfectly good chocolates is a sign, "Have one." (They will leave them alone, probably, thinking there's something wrong.)

A Herald assembles Royal Court, calling for all to make way for King, give him Royal Welcome. He enters wearing rubber boots, colored raincoat as cape, indifferently made crown, umbrella as scepter. Beating of pans (and playing of improvised orchestra with combs) welcomes him. He sits on throne, holds out his scepter and blesses all, and calls on Jester to take charge.

ROYAL MARCH. Participants do grand march and other active and musical games, retitled appropriately.

ROYAL GAMES. Equipment games (with titles over them), retitled party games.

ROYAL MAGIC, STUNTS. Whatever has been prepared will be fun.

ROYAL MUSIC. Group singing or Royal Band playing. Musical gags would be appropriate.

ROYAL DRAMA. Skits, especially of foolish nature.

ROYAL FOOD. Refreshments.

ROYAL FINISH. Nice closing with songs, perhaps worship. This part to be serious.

HALLOWEEN
(Ages 9 to 90)

Shakespeare and his ghostly troupe
Invite you to join their group.
They'll tour the musty catacombs,
And give you thrills to chill your bones.

Most of fun of traditional Halloween party comes from effects: black cats, witches, scarecrows, ghosts, bats. Decorations are usually in keeping, along with painted graveyard scene on wall, dimly lit, spider webs, for instance. Here are some suggestions for effects at Halloween. (Don't make them too scary for young ones.)

Reception. At door by person in ghostly costume with wet rubber glove. Dim lights. Guests are taken to Chamber of Horrors, perhaps through some passage where they must stoop, and are hit in face by cobwebs (thread or yarn suspended from ceiling).

Chamber of Horrors. Witch receives, gives swat with broom. Person made to taste Witches' Brew (Kool-aid fortified with powdered alum). Hand rail is charged with electricity. Floor is strewn with boxes, egg shells, corn stalks, balloons, squeegy things. Dim light reveals corpse on bed, which may move a bit. Face, dimly lighted, has eyes of eggshells, which suddenly light up in dark. Skeleton or skull is painted with phosphorescent paint. Strange noises, groans, grunts, hootings. Ghost on stilts. Beheading, with sight of axe slowly descending, groan, spirit led to next room. Several voices in mournful voice recite together, "Caught by witches, caught by witches."

Costumes. It is well to insist on having people wear costumes. Try to discover who is who. Contest for most interesting, most horrible, most original, may be held, judging made from Witch Parade, in which all join.

Death of Mr. Digger. This may be part of Chamber of Horrors, or in dimly lighted room. Story is told of death of Mr. Digger (substitute name) and his parts are passed around for all to feel: rubber glove with sand for hand, spools for spine, grapes for eyes, macaroni for windpipe, wet sponge for brains, calf's liver for liver, weiners for intestines.

Grand March, Musical Games. Done to ghostly music. Have people fly like bats, walk like ghosts, hoot like owls, screech like witches, groan, during Grand March, which may be soft dirge music.

Active Games. Use relays, active games, with apples for objects to be passed, also games like Pass It On, Hot Potato (using apples).

Skill Games. Toss bean bags into Witches' Pot; throw darts at black cats; rework or retitle—and you have new game.

CHRISTMAS PARTY
(Ages 9 to 90)

Invitations might be done on miniature Christmas trees, Santas, stars. (Each is to bring gift, perhaps something he has made.) When guests arrive, they make themselves name tags on appropriate material, such as construction paper, with crayons or new ball-point paints, in tubes. They also might be put to work to make for themselves special caps or other Christmas costumes. Each has bell to put on his cap.

Musical Games. Jingle Bells is a natural, of course, to get started. Grand Marches can be done to Christmas music.

Games. Game of Telegram could be used. Have each person make out telegram beginning with letters in CHRISTMAS or KRIS KRINGLE. See Star Tracing. Use Doodles, with people drawing Christmasy things. Drawing in Dark (draw Santa, his sleigh, his reindeer, a moon in sky). Reindeer Racing Game (see Turtle Racing Game) would be fun. Also Bell Pass, Snow Modeling, Confetti Pictures (Christmas theme), Balloon Games. Pin the Pack on Santa's Back (old Pin the Tail on the donkey, adapted). (To locate the games, check the index for each name.) Don't use all— select some. Near end, play music, pass all presents around seated circle, and see who got what.

Songs. Carols and popular songs are always good at Christmas time, especially if around a fire. Turn room lights out with candles aglow instead of hearth fire. It gives warm glow. Close (after refreshments) with quiet carol, prayer for peace and good will.

SOME OTHER CHRISTMAS IDEAS

Here are some further ideas which will appeal to all ages:

Christmas Neighborhood Party. In homes in neighborhood, invite in neighbors or, in organizations, have series of home parties on same evening, in homes all over town.

Toy Repair Party. Bring and repair toys. This may extend over more than one session.

Craft Time for Christmas. People come together and do simple crafts for Christmas presents. Especially good for children. See craft books and the Christmas edition of many magazines for Christmas craft ideas.

Holly Day Bazaar. A church invited people to come and buy gifts at St. Nick's Nook for their holly-days: holly-woods, holly-dollys, holly-foods, holly-goods, holly-bibs. Another year it held Santa Claus Fair.

Ornament-Making Party. Near Christmas time, a student group in one college serves pot pies. After supper each student washes pie tin and cuts ornaments from it with scissors for group Christmas tree. They have colors of quick-drying paint, string, scotch tape, ribbon, nail polish.

Christmas Tree Lighting. Some groups like to have ceremony for lighting of Christmas tree, for home, group, or community.

Decorating Ingenuity. Chicken feeder or water trough, painted, makes interesting centerpiece. Poultry wire can be cut into bell shape, or formed into cornucopia. Beat with rotary beater 1 cup Ivory Snow and 1/2 cup water until fluffy, for snow. To silver objects, pour silver paint on top of water and submerge object, drawing it up slowly through paint. It will be coated with silver.

Christmas Caroling. Caroling party may be held, starting from church or other center, moving out to sing for families, shut-ins, children's homes, nursing homes, returning to get some coffee or chocolate after couple of hours.

Decorating Tree. This might be party for smaller group, either making decorations and decorating tree, or buying decorations and finishing job, singing while working.

SPACE PARTY
(For older children, youth, adults)

This Space Party was done in Methodist Youth Camp. For atmosphere, advance announcements were made, "Listen to this important announcement," followed by slow speed tape played on recorder at fast speed so that voices were high, unintelligible. "Listen for further announcements" was followed by tape played on rewind so that it sounded like rocket ship.

At supper meeting leaders came in, dressed in Space Costumes. One wore green bathing cap and green swim suit, and painted his entire body green. Another got two rubber false faces and had a face front and back. They were brought in with space ship sounds (rewind on tape recorder).

Decorations were flying saucers (two paper plates put together). Volley-balls, globes, were hung around to represent planets, some of them marked. Games were renamed, like "The Flying Saucer Polka."

PLANS FOR A CIRCUS
(All ages)

One of the best affairs of all to use large numbers of people is an amateur circus. It may be elaborate or simple; rehearsed or almost spontaneous. Everybody can find something to do as animals, barkers, band members, ringmaster, sideshow operators, skill game operators.

It is important to have colorful atmosphere, circus music, lots of animals, and a big parade, if possible. A very large circus might actually involve dozens and dozens of performers, while small one might involve 15-25. With 45 minutes to one hour available, a miniature improvised circus may be worked out, dividing crowd into five or six groups and assigning role to each one—such as band, animal act, side show. (This is particularly good in camps where people can run to cabins and get properties.)

Making the Animals. It is not hard to devise realistic-looking animals. Heads and necks are often formed of chicken wire, covered with cloth or newspaper or toweling, dipped in paste, like paper mâché, and painted when dry.

Paper sacks of various sizes, blankets, brooms, and shorter sticks are combined to make animal raw material; blanket to cover two players forming most animals; broom or stick for the neck, paper sacks for heads and tied-on feet (especially for elephants) to make footwork look realistic. Belts or broad cords or ropes can become tails, rubber hose for elephant's nose. Newspapers are good for stuffing. Pajamas stuffed can be costume for many animals. Some can use wooden hoops.

The Ringmaster. He supervises all—acts, trainers, animals. Has top hat, cutaway or riding boots and pants and whip, whistle to call the plays. He introduces acts and encourages applause at proper time. He may give band its cue to play or stop playing.

The Band. Improvised instruments are good. Band plays under direction of costumed director, and may itself be costumed. Records may be used for atmosphere.

Spectaculars for the Big Top

1. Cowboys and Indians, or rodeo procedure, with trick riding of stick horses or improvised horses made of two boys with blanket over them and fancy heads. Lassoing.
2. Mass dance—Spanish, Indian, and so on.
3. Trick riding acts.
4. Chariot race, pulled by humans with human rider.
5. Bull fight, with all pageantry of bull fighting, using improvised bull.
6. Band parading, using combs, kazoos, clicking scissors, beating on wastebaskets.
7. Animal parade, elephants, each holding to tail of elephant ahead; lions in cages, bears dancing along on chains held by keepers, and the like.

Animal Acts. Lions can roar, step up on stool as directed by trainer (armed with chair). Kangaroos can box. Elephants can count by pawing. Seals can balance balls or balloons on their noses, swim around. (This they would pantomime with their "flippers.") Trained dogs can climb or bark numerals. Peculiarly devised aniimals, like dragons, cattywampuses, can perform acts.

Clown Stunts

1. Run over by steam roller. Fashion steam roller from large cardboard boxes, and have it manned by clowns. It runs over clown (who gets up under it) and leaves his flattened clothes on floor.
2. High dive. Clown on high place is supposed to dive into bucket of water. He motions his assistant to right, to left, but never dives.
3. Tight rope act. With rope on ground or floor, clown on each end holding it, third clown does tight rope act.
4. Surgery. Clown is knocked out. Other clowns pantomime trouble, get doctor (who may have his name on him, "Dr. Quack").
   First test is to tickle him with feather (test his sense of humor).
   Next is to tickle bottom of feet. (Dead or alive?)
   Then step on him. (See if he's breathing.)
   Raise his hands. (He squirts water from his mouth.)

Knock on his knees. (Test his IQ.)
And any other tests that clowns can devise.
Finally he gets up and goes off by himself.
5. Patent medicine act. Clown with umbrella under clothes, who can gain or lose weight on taking patent medicine by raising or lowering the umbrella.
6. Volunteer fire brigade. If safe to do it, use smoke pots, and child's wagon for the fire engine. Clowns are very inefficient. Fire engine could be made by old automobile stunt, with clown grasping ankles for each tire. Tire goes flat on way, must be fixed. Ladders, ladies' hose, other gags may be worked in.
7. Comic character clowns. Keep doing acts in keeping with their characters.
8. The filled auto stunt. Either real or imitation very small auto is driven up and many clowns get out—more than normally expected.
9. Operation stunt. This is done behind sheet, and garden hose (for intestines), cardboard knives, tin can are used. Punch line sometimes used: "A can, sir," holding one up.
10. Policeman stunt. Two clowns stage mock fight or holdup, are arrested by another. They take his stick from him and drive him off the scene.
11. Kiddy car clowns. They drive as in traffic, perhaps with policeman.
12. Clown juggler. He juggles some unlikely objects.
13. Trick shirt. Can be made or bought. The tail is 15 to 20 feet long, stuffed down in clown's pants. One clown grasps one shoulder of shirt, another the other, and they pull it over his head.
14. Other clown acts are things like looking for lost articles, finally finding them; chasing each other for cause or not;leap frog with variations; other athleticlike acts; playing silly musical instruments; handling a dangerous animal in casual manner. Also, lassoing, and strong man act (small clown carries off several weights which strong clown has hefted). Anything very small (like toy wagon) or of exaggerated size may be used by clowns. (They should not detract from other acts, but do theirs between times.)
15. Clown bull fight, with two clowns being bull (with blanket over them).
16. "Eats and sleeps under water." Clowns indicate by gestures and perhaps by signs that this marvel eats and sleeps under water. They hold a glass or jar of water above him. (See also Side Show Ideas.)

Side Show Ideas

1. The Fat Lady—stuffed with pillows.
2. The Knife Eater—he eats with his knife.
3. Zaza, the Bearded Lady—with an obviously attached beard, even a mop.
4. Siamese Twins—two girls in one dress.
5. The Cancan—two tin cans.
6. Two-Headed Man—two heads coming from one coat (one might be painted balloon).
7. Snake Charmer—he works on human snake that wriggles about.
8. The Strong Man—lifts heavy weights, with arms and teeth, bends hose.
9. Swimming Match—match swimming in water.
10. Water Color Exhibition—twenty glasses of colored water.
11. Headless, Hairless Dog—wiener.
12. Invisible Fish—bowl full of water.

13. For Men Only—display of toilet articles.
14. For Women Only—same. (Costs twice as much to get in wrong one.)
15. Headless Hydra—sponge.
16. Flying Red Bat—brickbat, suspended from ceiling.
17. Peep Show—mirror.
18. Palm Read—she drops mercurochrome in your palm.
19. Ancient Instrument of Punishment—worn slipper.
20. Bonaparte—two bones, apart.
21. Real Diamond Pin—dime and pin.
22. Drive Through the Wood—nail driven through wood.
23. Knight of the Bath—card marked "Saturday."
24. Cherry-Colored Cat—black cat.
25. Midget—child in grown-up clothing, or person with head and arms through a sheet, hands in some shoes resting on table.
26. Remains of Ancient Greece—candle holder, burnt candle.
27. Ruins of China—broken cup, saucer.
28. Watch on the Rhine—watch on an orange rind.
29. Unusual 25-Carat Ring—25 carrots, in ring.
30. Half Man, Half Woman—man side has hairy chest, sock, garter, man's shoe. Woman side has half wig, lipstick, eye shadow, earring, half dress, Nylon stocking, high heel shoe, bracelets.
31. Beauty and the Beast—girl dressed attractively; beast formed by two boys, blanket, special head. May be lion, tiger. It performs.
32. Bust of Blue Boy—pair of blue overalls, busted out at seat.
33. Bridle Scene—bridle on wall or chair.
34. Fatima, the Fan Dancer.
35. Northern Lights—have corner of room marked North, lights located there.
36. Total Eclipse—room goes completely dark.
37. The Wild Man—with savage face and tusks.
38. Horse with His Head Where His Tail Ought to Be—his tail is in the food end of manger.
39. Aladdin and His Lamp—fellow with sign on him, "Al. Addin." His lamp is beside him.
40. Puppet Show—have short one.
41. Trip Around the World—take them around the world (globe) and have something to trip over.
42. The Giant—person with umbrella over head, who raises umbrella to become fat.
43. Birth of a Nation—chairs made up with blankets like pullman berth, with sign "Pullman" over them.
44. Tattooing—done with piece of ice, with victim not looking.

Concessions

1. Fortune teller—she actually tells fortunes.
2. Turkey shoot—darts thrown at target, marked for prizes.
3. Tossing objects into a barrel—free prizes for successful tosses.
4. Bowling—croquet balls, rolled at tenpins.
5. The grab bag—grab without looking.

6. Shooting gallery—with pop gun or water pistol.
7. Hit the clown—throw cotton balls at clown's face (or other soft object).
8. Grocery store—where you can buy objects.
9. Post office—where, for small fee, you can get lovely love letter.
10. Airplane ride—person is blindfolded after stepping on board, which is held by person on each end, lifted few inches off the floor. He has hand on head of person, who slowly goes into knee bend, giving impression of rising in air.
11. Almost any of the Equipment and Skill Games—see Chapter 8.

FOOTBALL PARTY
(For youth and adults)

Decorations. In the colors chosen for opposing teams—outlandish combinations such as violet and green, or red and orange.

Personnel. Each side needs 5 players, captain, 2 to 5 substitutes, coach, waterboy, doctor, cheer leader, band (one for each side or one combined band), referee, scorekeeper, timekeeper. (The referee really directs the party.)

Refreshments. Hot dogs and lemonade or pop, or hot chocolate, popcorn, apples.

Some Equipment and Properties

1. Badges made from strips of crepe paper pinned behind small cardboard card, given to guests as they come. All who are not players become rooters.
2. Pennants for each side. (Triangular pieces of crepe paper pinned or pasted on small stick.)
3. Mimeographed sheets with songs and yells.
4. Band instruments, including combs with tissue paper folded over them.
5. Buckets of water and towels for water boys; medicine case for doctor; watch or clock for timekeeper; whistle for referee, blankets for players on bench.
6. Large colored paper numbers (pasted on cardboard to make them stiffer) pinned on each player's back. Books in shoulders for padding.
7. Bean bag or other tossed object for football.
8. Diagram chalked on floor (approximately 6' × 4', like illustration.)
9. Line of scrimmage chalked about 10' from the playing field. Progress of ball indicated on scoreboard or blackboard.

```
                    GOAL
        10 |                      |  10
        20 |                      |  20
        30 |                      |  30
        40 |                      |  40
        50 |                      |  50
        40 |                      |  40
        30 |                      |  30
        20 |                      |  20
        10 |                      |  10
           |        GOAL          |
```

Description of Game (Reds vs. Blues)

1. Crowd arrives for football party, is divided into two sides, who choose nicknames and elect personnel mentioned above, if it has not been done in advance.
2. Each side has 20 to 30 minutes to get ready, including decorating, cheers, songs.
3. At signal, entire Red team gallops out in best football manner, warms up and exercises, facing bleachers of their side. Bleachers are chairs arranged in rows. Playing field (allow 10 to 12 foot width) is between the two sets of bleachers. Reds sit on their bench. Blues exercise, then sit, as Reds did.
4. Referee calls forth two captains for toss. He tosses coin. Winner plays first.
5. Each team, in rotation and within time limits, gets four pitches with ball. Game is played by pitching bean bag onto diagram. Ball starts on own 40-yard line as game opens and for second half.
6. Ball is put into play from behind line of scrimmage as players go into huddle, decide who will pitch it to diagram. Plays are to look like regular football, and regular rules are used where applicable. Quarters are best at 8 minutes, 6, 5, 4, as interest lags.
7. Spectators are seated in bleachers, rows of chairs facing playing field. Referee is really director of party.
8. Much originality is called for. Referee makes up rules as he goes along; coaches argue with him; players get hurt and doctor and nurse patch them up; there is a snake dance at the half, and crowning of King and Queen.
9. Victory Celebration could include songs, group games, or folk games. Refreshments are sometimes served during game, and sometimes after entire party.
10. Referee uses his judgment in all cases. Each side must make touchdown in four downs or surrender ball. Therefore, first team to play must make 60 yards.
11. Sometimes this party is put on by bringing all materials necessary and having two sides start from scratch to name teams, choose queen, and so on, as part of party itself. Sometimes it is planned in advance.

ONE WORLD PARTY
(For older children, youth, adults)

This one world idea was used outdoors by a group of 250 young people in a summer conference, and may have to be adapted if you use it. With some changes, it could be used indoors.

At first the idea was to have either an Airplane or a World Friendship Party. Instead, the ingenious committee decided to put the two ideas together, and make it an outdoor party. They did, and this is the result.

Pilot Training. First there was the pilot training one afternoon. Then there were mimeographed tickets, distributed to each of 250 travelers. Flight assignments were made on tickets themselves. Passengers gathered at the airport, where public address system had been set up. Here each pilot was given his wings by chairman in elaborate ceremony. Soon flights were called.

Your Flight Is Ready. Voice of announcer called over speaker system, "Passengers holding space on Flight 1, please report to runway." All who held tickets for this flight went to runway, where their trained pilot awaited them at plane. Outline of plane was made by two cotton strings, laid out like illustration. Pilot placed himself at head, at position of propeller. Each passenger was instructed to reach down, take hold of string, stand again, and hold on tight. (Appearance of group, then, was something like that of plane.)

(Outline of plane)

"Pilot Jones, your runway is clear," said loud speaker. Pilot Jones then began to make noises like airplane engine (as per his instructions in training during afternoon) and all *ran* together down *run*way, to first stop.

Stops were made at shows depicting (either humorously or seriously) life in many countries around world. Other flights were called in similar manner, until all were soon flying. Pilots had had their instructions as to order in which they were to make various shows.

"Gay Paree" represented France. It was special show devised by all-male cast. Boys put on what they called French Revue. India was represented by snake charmer. China was represented. Hawaii was presented by one of girls, dressed in grass skirt, singing Hawaiian songs. For Africa, group did verse speaking arrangement of Vachel Lindsey's rhythmic poem, "The Congo." (This group was seated around fire like Africans.) Then there was The Valley of Nun (nobody there) and Shangri-la (refreshments). The group came together to the airport to sing international songs in closing.

Variations of this can be developed easily. Each plane might fly to a specific city— Moscow, Tokyo, London, Berlin, Rome, Prague, Sao Paulo, Mexico City. Then each group could work out a dramatization in keeping with the people who live in that city, and enact the playlet for the entire group. The plane could become a train or trolley. One group took a tour around town by projecting kodachrome scenes on cheesecloth in the background, and then putting on acts appropriate for that section of town.

NEW YEAR'S EVE PARTY—Turn Over a New Leaf
(For youth and adults)

Planning to turn over a new leaf on January 1st? Come to . . . .
. . . . at 9:00 P.M., Dec. 31.
Bring along something you'd like to get rid of besides your bad habits.
Wrap it in mystery.

Hand each guest leaf-shaped tag with his name on one side and, on other, written resolution which he must put into effect at once at party. Suggestions: To talk about my heavy income tax whenever I can find anyone to listen to me; to speak affectionately to all girls during entire evening; to say "Sir" or "Ma'am" whenever spoken to; to count up to ten before answering any questions; to bow before addressing lady; to give pump-handle shake to all with whom I speak; to brag about my ancestors to everyone.

Give guests thirty beans apiece. Every time they are caught breaking their good resolutions they must pay penalty of one bean to the person who catches them in act. At close of evening the one with most beans might be presented with diploma of merit for keeping his resolutions.

Swap. Get out mysterious packages which have been brought and deposited on arrival in large box. Each takes package at random and starts to swap—using beans for money. Announce that special recognition will be given at end of game to one who has possession of largest package, smallest package, and one who collects most beans. Wrappings must not be removed until game ends. Package must be swapped each time to make sure that no one corners the booty, for each should have one package at end. To have most fun unwrapping, we suggest that all sit in circle, and one at time display his swap.

Advice. Give each guest slip of paper on which is to be written bit of advice. Have the slips folded up and collected. After mixing them up, pass out to each, one at time. As each receives his slip, he will stand, state what he thinks of advice and what he intends to do about it, and then, and not until then, will he open slip and read aloud what is written there. Suppose John Jones has said advice is excellent and that he will carry it out to best of his ability; then he reads, "You should get up at 5:00 every morning and make Hungarian goulash for breakfast."

Father Time. Divide guests into teams of five to ten, depending on size of your group. Line up each team facing large sheet of paper on wall or screen. On chair beside paper place large black crayon, and number of slips of paper placed upside down, containing names of items to be drawn; two each of ears, eyes, arms, hands, and feet; robed body, nose, mouth, beard, hair, and name "Father Time." At signal each player runs up, takes slip, and draws feature named. Masterpieces of art resulting from this method will prove highly entertaining.

Resolutions. Give each guest slip of paper on which he will write resolution which he is making for the new year. No names are to be signed. When these are collected have them read for crowd to call out guess as to who wrote each one.

New Year's Greetings. With good march being played, get all into couples for grand march in circle. There should be one extra person at least who stands in center of circle. If there are enough men to make good number of couples, they should form marching circle, and all extra women should stand in center. Men march in outer circle, if they are smaller number. At each blow of whistle, inner circle reverses and marches in opposite direction. Outer circle always moves in same direction. When two circles are moving in opposite directions extra players get in line and march with inner circle. At blow of whistle inside circle again reverses and marches with outer circle. When they do this each person in inner circle tries to get partner. As each catches hands of partner (skating position), he greets other with "Hi, partner!" Outside circles does not slow up, but keeps moving in time to music. Again players without partners go to center. Use such songs as "O Susanna," "Polly Wolly Doodle," and "Old Zip Coon" for music.

This is time to lead marching circles past serving window for refreshments, or to places around long tables. The latter is particularly nice, for the time following fellowship of eating together might appropriately be spent singing, finally leading up to a high spiritual plane as midnight approaches. Many groups will want to have some special service in the sanctuary at this time; others may want simply to stand with bowed heads as clocks strike twelve, while someone reads:

"We have been joking together tonight about turning over a new leaf and making good resolutions, but let us be serious now as we pray:

> Oh, make me glad, dear Lord, that every passing day
>   Brings a clean page in thy book of life;
> A chance to turn the blotted pages down
>   And start again, refreshed for the great strife.
>
> Teach me to turn each bitter fault and grief
>   Into a lesson that may prove a guard
> Against temptation, and the bitter foes
>   That lie in wait and press the fighter hard.
>
> Teach me to see the little joys of life,
>   The beauty of the world each passing day;
> Teach me wide sympathy and tenderness,
>   That in the end I may most humbly say:
>
> "There are some pages, Lord, both clean and white,
>   Writ with good deeds, with sunshine, and with cheer:
> That Thou may'st put into my eager hands
>   Thy book of days to make a better year."

AUTHOR UNKNOWN

Learn the song, "All Night, All Day," and use for closing.

DECORATING

Many people like to use natural decorations as much as possible—such as leaves, branches, cornstalks, flowers. However, the artificial will add color. Many craft stores feature a number of inexpensive booklets showing decoration ideas for parties and banquets, as well as demonstrating how to make flowers, favors, place cards for all kinds of social affairs.

Planning Banquet, Mealtime Fun

3

One of the greatest means of creating fellowship in the human race is the experience of eating together, particularly if the act can be made an enjoyable occasion through entertainment and fun. And this holds true whether the meal is a groaning banquet table or a supper of pancakes and sausage in somebody's big kitchen. However, when people are sitting beside each other who have not been previously acquainted, there can be awkward, uncomfortable times unless those in charge have thoughtfully provided icebreakers, as suggested in the later section on informal mealtime fun.

This chapter give also tips for the toastmaster at a formal banquet. It lists with brief descriptions some thirty kinds of banquets that might be planned, and nine seasonal banquet briefs. Then there are detailed plans for seven other unusual banquets, and finally full suggestions for a mother-daughter and a father-son banquet.

THE TOASTMASTER
(See also "Master of Ceremonies," Chapter 1)

The toastmaster is the go-between chairman. He represents the group present in handling the program, he represents the planning committee and its ideas, and he is the one who may have a relationship to the kitchen about service details after the banquet has begun.

His job is to keep the affair moving in progressive, easy style. He is to know and introduce the performers, acquaint them with anything they need to know. The toastmaster should give all the performers such a background and build-up that each will feel at ease and be eager to do his best. (This rules out over- and under-emphasis on the personality, standing, and accomplishments of the performer.)

The toastmaster keeps things pleasant with humorous remarks, jokes, even gags. Here too an overdose is not desirable. If such padding is not needed by him, even though he preplanned it, the best toastmaster will pass up his opportunity to shine in order to allow his performers to do it.

He not only introduces program people, but recognizes honored guests, making appropriate remarks as they are presented to the entire group. He spreads the limelight judiciously.

A toastmaster must deal with the timing and length of the program. It is his job to cut things short (not always a pleasant task) when they get too long. The guests should be able to leave saying, "I'm glad I came!"

Some General Suggestions to Toastmasters

1. Have the program worked out in advance, written on cards. Remarks too may be written on cards, to be placed aside when you are finished with them.

2. Prepare more remarks than you will need. Be ready for the unexpected. Consider in advance what you will do if the speaker or a main program performer does not show up.
3. You may have a bite or two in advance, only appearing to eat. A good many toastmasters cannot enjoy the meal, even if it be a good one, because of the coming responsibility.
4. Try to put yourself in the position of members of the group. Watch them carefully. Is the room too hot, too cold? Have it adjusted. Are they tired? Have a stretcher for them. (See Stretchers, Chapter 4.)
5. Read the mealtime fun helps for some ideas for getting participation at the tables. After the invocation, for instance, ask the group to exchange humorous remarks with each other. Tell of a few you've heard. (See Chapter 5.)
6. Be prepared with several jokes that have a point related to the occasion. "Some of you know that our committee had considerable difficulty in getting this affair together. We had so many ups and downs that we felt like the elevator operator who muttered to himself, 'I'm not a man. I'm a yo-yo!' "

Sample Program. After the Invocation, you may want to warm up the group with some group starter idea or conversation stimulator. (If it is an athletic affair, have them tell the roughest time they ever had in a game.)

After the meal, ask the groups to share something that occurred at their table during the conversation (if the banquet is not too large). This is a good time for some group singing, toasts. Take up items of business as quickly as possible. Entertainment and other program items come now—solos, quartets, acts.

Then comes the introduction of the speaker or the main event on the program. Now is the time for honoring, awards, presentations, done with proper ceremony but not too much flourish. End with a rousing patriotic song, group sing, hymn. Religious groups will generally have a benediction. Dismissal may be otherwise with some fairly serious thought to take away with them: a thought for the day.

Stopping the Long-Winded. The greatest single problem of the toastmaster is keeping the affair within the time limits. This is particularly true of speakers. Here are a few suggestions that might work:

1. If you know the speaker well, you might say: "I know George Harper very well. We want to school together. He asked me what he should speak about, and I suggested about 20 minutes. When I shake my watch, he is to quit."
2. Another way more delicate might be to say, "Some of our group must leave at 9 o'clock, Dr. Longwind, I happen to know, and they have told me they want to hear all of your speech. I'll notify you when you have five more minutes."
3. Pass the speaker a note, saying "We must be through in five more minutes."
4. Perhaps with the help of some stooges (if your speaker is a notorious forgetter) lead an extra long applause, thank him, and move on.
5. Simply thank him (even though he is not through) when he has finished a soliloquy, and say pleasantly but firmly, "Our agreement was to be through by 9 o'clock, and we have reached that time. We want to thank Mr. or Mrs. So-and-so for this thought-provoking address, and we know you will want to come forward to talk with him/her."

No one likes to be rude, but you may be the only hope the group has of getting home before midnight. Remember that you are its representative! Do it graciously, but *do it!*

Widsom for the Toastmaster. Some of these humorous little quips may sometime find a natural niche in the toastmaster's remarks. (See also "When to Use Humor", Chapter 5)

A hair on the head is worth two in the brush.

The bigger a man's head gets, the easier it is to fill his shoes!

Happiness is not absent—we just don't recognize its presence!

Try enlarging upon your blessings as you enlarge upon your troubles!

"We do not stop playing because we grow old. We grow old because we stop playing."—HERBERT SPENCER.

Wallflowers are the people left when the popular ones and their popular friends consort together.

Many a man who is a big bug at the office is little more than an insect when he gets home.

"The best way to cheer yourself is to try to cheer somebody else up."—MARK TWAIN.

It's not the hours you put into your work, but the work you put into your hours.

Don't waste time reflecting on missed opportunities. While reflecting you might miss some more!

Any old fish can float downstream. It takes a live fish to swim up.

Be kind to people as you climb the ladder of success—you may meet them again on the way down!

Three rules for avoiding criticism completely: (1) Say nothing, (2) do nothing, (3) be nothing.

For the courageous, each failure is a new starting point.

To be born a gentleman is an accident—to die one is an achievement.

Is is not what we eat but what we digest that makes us strong.
Is is not what we gain but what we save that makes us rich.
Not what we read but what we remember that makes us learned,
Not what we profess but what we practice that makes us religious.

—BACON

"Some children are on the streets at night because they are afraid to stay home alone."

When you point your finger at someone else's guilt or shortcomings, have you noticed that you have three fingers pointing at yourself?

"Men will argue for religion, fight for it, die for it, anything but live for it."—ANON.

You get ulcers more from what's eating on you than from what you eat.

The most underdeveloped territory in the world is right under your hat.

There are better ways of getting up in the world than hitting the ceiling!

SOME TYPES OF BANQUETS

If you are looking for an excuse to hold a banquet, perhaps some one of these nearly thirty types of banquets will give you one. (See also "Party Idea Starters", Chapter 2.)

Brotherhood Banquet. In celebration of Brotherhood Week.

Tribute Banquet. To someone who has achieved, served well, perhaps is retiring. Special songs for the person, special speeches, gifts, are in order.

TV Banquet. For program, several TV features could be imitated, such as quiz shows, news, comedy shows, variety presentations, hillbilly music.

Graduation Banquet. Complete with processional, high-class music, Last Will, Honor Graduates (who perform), Alma Mater.

Under the Big Top. This features circus, of course, with animal decorations, balloons, miniature tents at tables. Acts could perform there (if there is room) or in another spot or outdoors. Each table could be asked to decorate its own (from materials furnished) and to do circus act.

Melting Pot Banquet. Each table represents different country. Before banquet there is tour of the world. Program has international flavor—songs, games, stories.

Mother Goose Mother-Daughter Banquet. To give a little variation, use this theme with Mother Goose decorations and program features. Don't let it get too sentimental.

Gay 90's Banquet. Decorations, songs and program, dress are in keeping. Eat by lamplight. Singing waiters. Wear your costumes. More fun for older youth and mixed adult groups than for younger folk.

Transportation Banquet (Railroad Days, Airplane, Ox Cart to Flying Saucer, Ocean Cruise). Select program and decorations to fit. Costumes for leaders or table waiters could be in keeping with theme, such as trainman's garb.

Gourmet Banquet. Either serve fancy food and have highbrow program, or serve corned beef hash and have lowbrow program. Older groups more interested in this.

Rainbow Banquet. Decorate with all colors, including balloons. Songs like Over the Rainbow; have Pot of Gold Quiz.

Indoor Camping Banquet. Decorate tables appropriately, have camplike program.

Artists Banquet. Decorate with artists theme. For program have some artists perform. Let each person at table create work of art in paints, clay, crayolas, paper.

Musical March of Time. Program features music as it has been done through centuries, and how it will be done in A.D. 3,000.

Book Banquet. Each person comes representing book title. Book characters from well-known works are represented in program. Have book quiz. A talk on values of reading, or how to enjoy book.

Kid Banquet. Everyone tries to recapture days of their youth.

Turnabout Banquet. Men come dressed as women, women as men. Both act their roles. "Battle of the Sexes" quiz.

Starvation Banquet. Short meal is served, money taken for world relief. Program may be lighthearted or serious.

Recognition Banquet. To honor some person, or to represent progress of group. Go back into history and bring things up to date.

Harvest Home Banquet. Have folk come dressed in old-fashioned clothes. Get them to make hats, bonnets when they come, from newspaper or colored paper. Cornucopias for tables.

Springtime Party. Features flowers, return of spring, "in the spring a young man's fancy turns to what the girls have been thinking of all winter."

Hobo Banquet. Decorations and food are in keeping. (Could be outdoor affair.) Eat from tin cans, sing hobo songs, tell stories.

Dinner in _____ (You fill in blank). This banquet could take banqueteers to any part of globe, such as Alaska, Scandinavia, South Sea Islands, Australia.

Comic Characters Banquet. Include any of comics. Skits represent comic characters. Each table might put on skit if there are not too many.

Gypsy Banquet. Decorations, atmosphere, songs, program are gypsyish.

Southern Plantation Banquet. Decorations, songs, program carry you back to ol' Virginny or Mississippi.

Doof and Nuf Banquet. "Food and fun" spelled backward—and banquet is that, served backward, people wear clothes backward, program is backward.

Organizational Banquet. Most organizations have banquet at some time to review achievements, celebrate milestone or progress, and to look ahead.

Decorations are usually in organization colors, motto on display, material of special emphasis at plates, program and speechifying directed toward furthering organizational purpose. Be sure to have some table fun along with serious stuff. Often a skit, some good group singing, humorous songs and performances send people away, glad they came.

SEASONAL BANQUET BRIEFS

Adam and Eve (New Year's Eve, that is). Banquet especially for couples, taking year in retrospect.

Rail Splitters Banquet. Decorations in keeping, and program too, in honor of Lincoln, Honest Abe.

Cherry Tree Banquet. Cherries featured in decorations, George Washington in program.

Hearts and Hatchets Banquet. Combination of Valentine's and George Washington's Birthday in decorations and program

Red, White and Blue Banquet. For Fourth of July.

Greenery Banquet. Everything green for St. Patrick's Day.

Turkey Tale Banquet. Especially for Thanksgiving.

Bright Star Banquet. For Christmas time. Be sure to use carols as part of program.

PLANS FOR SEVEN UNUSUAL BANQUETS

Around the World Flight Banquet. Seat belts are in seats. Decorations have colors of flags, planes. Stewardesses serve the meal. After the meal, the trip is made, via song, from country to country, using such a collection of national songs. Group singing combined with solos and special numbers move the group from place to place. Films, filmstrips may be inserted to give flavor.

Decorate each table for a different country. One group has a Blarney Stone on a table for the O'Kellys, O'Gradys, and so on; windmills and tulips for Holland. Eskimos made of cleansing tissues stood in front of upturned cereal boxes for Alaska. Ming trees represented China and Japan. A tribe of Seminole Indians sat together at the table decorated with bow and arrows, tomahawks, buffalo skin. Egypt had a tall pyramid. This banquet may be followed with a folk festival in another room.

Pirates' Aftermath. Decorations were seaweed from green crepe paper; octopuses from newspaper and paste (small ones on the tables, big one on trunk from Davy Jones' locker). Whales made of construction paper (black). King Neptune wore beard made of mop.

Around locker were gold coins (stones painted yellow). Davy Jones, toastmaster, wore skull and crossbones on chest and headpiece. The people were dressed as pirates. On the walls were sea monsters and hundreds of fish, cut and strung up, blown by fans. The program included singing, games, and contests adapted in name, quiz, balloon, and other games.

Birthday Banquet. Give each person his birthstone ring material, and he makes ring himself, using pipe cleaners for bands, construction paper, and glitter. Here is birthstone for each month:

January—garnet (deep red)	**August**—sardonyx (orange-red)
February—amethyst (purple)	**September**—sapphire (blue)
March—aquamarine (pale green)	**October**—opal (various colors)
April—diamond (crystal)	**November**—topaz (yellow)
May—emerald (deep green)	**December**—turquoise (blue-green)
June—pearl (white)	
July—ruby (red)	

Let guests talk about their rings, show to each other as conversation pieces. Each month may be asked to sit together and present something appropriate, with January forewarned that it is to have the invocation. Other features could take form of songs, stunts, performances, jokes, riddles.

In December, sing some Christmas carols. Little birthday present could be at each place, or have group swap presents.

Shining Stars Banquet (for athletes). Decorate with school colors and appropriate miniatures for football, basketball, baseball, track, with team nickname used prominently. If trophy has been won, have it ready to display (perhaps for first time).

Use outline of football or whatever ball is appropriate as shape of banquet program. Include in printed program menu and outline of program. Save athletic jokes and cartoons, and place them around on tables for athletes to enjoy. Get them to tell, while eating, funniest thing that ever happened in a game. An invocation will precede the meal. After the meal, have following features:

1. Welcome and response.
2. Music, perhaps including group singing.
3. Talks, as appropriate, by visiting speaker, coach, president or principal. If championship has been won, acknowledge this.
4. Skits, stunts (with laugh at some of things that have happened during past season) are good.
5. Magic, good puppet show, movies might be used.
6. Special music.
7. School song and, in some cases, benediction.

Our College Around the World. This was spring banquet of school whose students served around world. Program as printed read:

FELLOWSHIP (Greet your neighbor)
INVOCATION (The hymnic grace)

THE MEAL (Fresh food, canned dinner music)
WE SING TOGETHER (Music is the universal language)
FAMILY ALBUM (De-skeletonized, consisting of some of the fun and predictions that come at the end of every school year)
GARRETT AROUND THE WORLD (Some of the things that are being done by alumni)
THINGS THAT SHOULD HAVE BEEN SAID (but weren't until now—these were remarks of appreciation for student accomplishments and faculty labors)
GARRETT MEN'S CHOIR (Songs)
HYMN OF DEDICATION (By all)

Over the Garden Fence

TABLE DECORATION: Flower or vegetable on each table, buried in dirt. Tables were Rakers, Sprinklers, Busy Bees, Carrots, Beets, Onions, Potatoes, Jack-in-the-Pulpits, Petunias, Daisies, Tulips, Weeders.
GRACE: Led by Jack-in-the-Pulpits
During meal each table contributes verse, song, or skit about what they are representing. Sprinklers distribute milk and coffee, Busy Bees bring in food, Weeders carry out dirty dishes.
PROGRAM: Advice consists of their singing "Sweetly Sings the Donkey."
Song, "Mr. Rabbit."
Group of four songs dealing with gardening.
So-called lecture by an authority on gardening as follows:
INTRODUCTION: "And now we present Miss Horty Culture from the *Onion*versity of *Seed*attle."
MISS HORTY CULTURE:

On the subject of gardening I couldn't be worse
So I'll speak to you in blank—er, garden verse.

When planting potatoes, cut them crosswise
And before covering them up, please close their eyes.

Try to plant your tomatoes all in a row
You'll find them lots easier to hoe, hoe, hoe.

Your watermelon vine by the gate you should stick
So that strangers passing by can take their pick.

Carrots, onions, and celery too—
Plant them together—they'll be ready for stew.

As far as squash and rutabagas go
It won't be far enough for me, I know.

Don't worry about weeds, just build a high fence
And plant many flowers—doesn't that make sense?

And for gardening advice, in prose or in rhyme,
I suggest that you get an authority next time.

Ye Olde Englishe Christmas Dinner. Here is the detailed description of a Christmas banquet:

SINGERS—enter from the hall, singing "It Came upon the Midnight Clear." March around center dining table, singing "Hark, the Herald Angels Sing." Are seated.

PAGES (soft music)—enter with wreaths and hang over fireplace. Trip out for garlands and fasten up. Hang mistletoe in center of room, then hide.

JESTER—comes running in, in most unusual manner, stubs toe and falls, jumps up, and announces the Lord and Lady. Jester says, "Yo! Ho! the Lord and Lady come!" and gesticulates in such a manner that the audience understands that it should rise. Runs back and forth joyously.

LORD AND LADY AND GUESTS (soft music)—pages enter, carrying candles. Lord and Lady follow. Two guests follow. March up one side of table and down the other, back to places. All are seated. Pages stand behind Lord.

READER: "It was an old English custom as far back as the Crusades to celebrate Christmas in this manner, especially at the Lord's Court. Part of the ceremony was the Yule Log. Everyone treated the log with great respect as it was dragged in, bowed to it as it passed. The log must burn all night, and then what was left must be kept very carefully, because it was supposed to guard the house during the year."

Advent of the Yule Log (soft music)

Pages march from the Lord's table to the entrance and return with the woodsmen dragging the log (Jester rides on the log). The Lord and his guests treat the log with great respect, bowing as it passes by and as the woodsmen place it on the fire and light it. (Woodsmen stand by the fireplace.)

READER: "A ceremony of great importance was that of bringing in the boar's head. It was usually on a silver dish and decorated with lemons and greens. It was carried into the hall accompanied by trumpets and lighted candles. The custom originated at Queen's College, Oxford, and it is still observed there."

Advent of the Boar's Head (soft music)

Pages retire and return with cook, bearing the boar's head on silver tray (decorated with greens). The cook sings the "Boar's Head Song" as he brings it in, places head on table and goes out main entrance.

READER: "One Christmas Charles II and his men went forth to hunt a stag. When they returned they piled logs in the fireplace that they might warm themselves and then have a feast. As they were all enjoying the huge loin of beef, King Charles knighted the beef. It is always served at a Christmas feast in England."

Advent of the Loin of Beef (soft music)

Pages retire. Re-enter beside cook bearing loin of beef. (Exit cook.) Lord rises and draws his sword and says, "Sir Loin, I dub thee knight!")

READER: "Sometimes the loin of beef was accompanied with a Yorkshire pudding, raisins and figs that make us think of the East, spices to remind us of the gifts of the Magi, sweets and fruits—the best of everything was placed on the platter. Then over it all was put a cover of pastry, on which a star is drawn, like that the wise men saw. They called it Christ's cradle."

Advent of the Plum Pudding (soft music)

Pages and cook enter as before.

READER: "When the cloth was removed, the cook brought in a huge silver vessel of rare and curious workmanship which he placed before the Lord. Its appearance was hailed with delight, being the wassail bowl so renowned in Christmas festivity. Having raised it to his lips with a hearty wish of Merry Christmas to all present, he sent it humming round the table for everyone to follow his example, pronouncing it the "ancient fountain of good feeling where all hearts meet together."

Advent of the Wassail Bowl (soft music)

Pages and cook as before. Singers sing "Wassail Song" as cook enters. Lord rises, drinks from the bowl, and says, "I bid you all a merry, merry Christmas." Pages pass it to Lady and each guest.
CHRISTMAS DINNER—jester entertains by her wit and ridiculous things she makes others do and does herself. Singers and all guests sing carols at intervals during dinner—especially English ones.
MUMMER'S PLAY
ENGLISH FOLK DANCERS—followed by entire group participating in a folk dance.

TWO BANQUETS POPULAR WITH FAMILIES

Mother and Daughter Banquet. Favorite banquet idea is mother-daughter one. Other theme titles are sometimes used, such as Hen-Chick or Cat-Kitten. Clever ideas should be devised to keep such an affair from getting too sentimental. Use of skits and humor helps, also singing fun songs as well as sentimental songs. Little contests like mother and daughter who weigh least, who are youngest, mother with most daughters—all tend to keep program lighter.

Another idea would be to bring in some boys and men to perform for the program (and in exchange, girls and women will go to their father-son affair to perform). Cute puppet shows, solos, trios, demonstrations of dances, slides, movies, may be used, as well as group singing, reading of humorous material such as boners or Colonel Stoopnagle's nonsense, will add fun. See also "Informal Mealtime Fun" in this chapter for ideas, especially for ideas like tongue twisters done at table between mother and daughter, or boners.

Most mother-daughter affairs like to end on a serious note, with a prayer. Try closing with the group singing Malotte's "The Lord's Prayer."

Father and Son Banquet. (Also called Chip and Block Banquet, Dad-Lad, Senior-Junior.) Many organizations like to get fathers and sons together, once a year, for a banquet. After the invocation there will be food and fellowship at the table. Jokes, easy puzzles may be conversation starters at the table.

Here are some ideas for the program:

1. Have contest to see what father-son combination have the biggest differential in waist measure.
2. Which father and son look least alike?
3. Which father and son have greatest total chest expansion?
4. Which is oldest father-son combination? Youngest? Tallest? Heaviest? (Have a set of scales at hand.)
5. Contest by tables (or between candles) to see which group of father-sons can name most father-son combinations in history and in the Bible.
6. Have talk by father (who might quote "A Father's Ten Commandments" given below), a response by son (or someone else's son). Don't let them get too sentimental.
7. Quizzes are good for this group.
8. Skits and stunts, humorous readings like "What Is a Boy?" (which follows below) make good program features.
9. By all means have some good singing, both group singing by all and some special music, perhaps by a father and son.
10. A serious talk might be made about fathers or sons of the Bible, such as the Prodigal Son (Luke 15:11-19), the Loving Father (Luke 15:20-24), John 3:16.
11. Magicians and other entertainers, singers, puppeteers, movies, could be on program also.

Do not let program continue too long. Fathers and sons could go to another room for some games.

What is a Boy?

Boys come in assorted sizes, weights, and colors. They are found everywhere—on top of, underneath, inside of, climbing on, swinging from, running around or jumping to. Mothers love them, little girls hate them, older sisters and brothers tolerate them, adults ignore them, and Heaven protects them. A boy is Truth with dirt on its face, Wisdom with bubble gum in its hair, and the Hope of the future with a frog in its pocket.

A boy has the appetite of a horse, the digestion of a sword swallower, the energy of a pocket-size atomic bomb, the curiosity of a cat, the lungs of a dictator, the imagination of a Paul Bunyan, the shyness of a violet, the audacity of a steel trap, the enthusiasm of a firecracker, and when he makes something he has five thumbs on each hand.

He likes ice cream, knives, saws, Christmas, comic books, the boy across the street, woods, water (in its natural habitat), large animals, Dad, trains, Saturday mornings, and fire engines. He is not much for Sunday School, company, schools, books without pictures, music lessons, neckties, barbers, girls, overcoats, adults, or bedtime.

Nobody else is so early to rise or so late to supper. Nobody else can cram into one pocket a rusty knife, a half-eaten apple, three feet of string, an empty Bull Durham sack, two gumdrops, six cents, a slingshot, a chunk of unknown substance, and a genuine supersonic code ring with a secret compartment.

A boy is a magical creature—you can lock him out of your workshop, but you can't lock him out of your heart. You can get him out of your study, but you can't get him out of your mind. Might as well give up—he is your captor, your jailer, your boss, and your master—a freckle-faced, pint-sized bundle of noise. But when you come home at night with only the shattered pieces of your hopes and dreams, he can mend them with two magic words—"Hi, Dad!"[3]

A Father's Ten Commandments

I.   Thou shalt love thy son with all thy heart and hesitate not to show it. This is the first and great commandment.

II. Thou shalt not carry graven upon thy heart any love greater than this. Business, sports, pleasures shall all take secondary place, for God gave him to be a chum and pal unto thee.

III. Thou shalt not take the name of "Father" upon thee lightly, for God will not hold him guiltless who hath little regard for the responsibilities of Fatherhood.

IV. Remember thy son's portion of thy time and keep it sacred for his use. Many days shalt thou labor and do all manner of work to provide suitably for his needs, but in that portion of thy day which belongeth to him thou shalt not do any work, neither shalt thou bury thy nose in a book, betake thyself to the golf links or seek thine own pleasure otherwise.

V.   Honor thy wife, my mother, for I, thy son, love her dearly and cannot admire, respect, and love thee if thou display not love toward her.

VI. Thou shalt counsel and advise with thy son in all things and share with him the secrets of thy heart.

VII. Thou shalt be firm in thy discipline, lest thy son stray away from the paths of righteousness for the lack of thy guiding hand. Not too tightly or too loosely shalt thou hold the rein of authority, but so that thy child shall recognize the wisdom of his father in life.

VIII. Thou shalt trust thy son and have patience with him for all his shortcomings, remembering that in thy boyhood others had so to do with thee.

IX. Thou shalt walk uprightly before all men, for thy child doth trust thee before all thers. Moreover, if thou shalt shake his confidence in thee it will not be lightly regained.

X.   Thou shalt not forget that thou wert once a boy, neither be unmindful that times have changed much since the days of thy youth.[4]

INFORMAL MEALTIME FUN
(Luncheon club—camp—church supper)

Here are some fun ideas to brighten the mealtime programs of groups in any situation short of a formal banquet.

Group Singing After Meals. Most people do not like to sing during meal, though they will sing between courses.

Decorating Own Table. If tables are assigned in advance, group may have much fun decorating its own table. Such materials as flame-proof crepe paper, construction paper, balloons, colored straws, flowers, colored leaves, greenery such as evergreens and magnolia leaves or Spanish moss, cotton, candles, bowls of fruit for cornucopia, souvenirs from foreign lands, may be used. For place cards, such materials as cards, cut-outs, bits of leaves, bark, branches, feathers, felt, cork, cloth, postage stamps, beads, crayolas, construction paper, sprigs of pine, hemlock, or holly, lollypops, aluminum and other foils, milk bottle caps, cardboard tubing, paper plates, doilies, gumdrops, raisins, figs, dates, dried seeds (beans, rice, peas), alphabet spaghetti, paste, scissors. From whatever materials are furnished, each is to construct his own. Have them show their wares to their own table, neighboring tables.

Decorating to a Theme. Place cards, nut cups, centerpieces, and all the rest are in keeping. Assign several families to decorate for family affair. Much fun can be had with animal themes for tables.

Imaginary Decorations. As suggested for other social affairs, person blessed with vivid imagination might paint picture (mental, that is) of beautifully decorated table, groaning with good things to eat. (Then bring out bologna sandwiches!)

Group Starters, Conversation Starters. Right after the invocation, have everybody talk about same thing, such as an embarrassing moment, best joke they've heard recently, what can you do to reduce 10 pounds, tricks for managing children, biggest deception ever pulled on you, hardest thing you have to do.

Graces for the Table. Get members of group to collect some for group use. Perhaps also to be mimeographed to be taken home.

Jokes, Knock-Knocks, Humorous Material on the Table. At each person's plate have a joke, knock-knock, silly song title, or other humorous material. Have everyone read them aloud at their tables, select best to be read to entire group. (Gets multiple participation— good conversation starter.) Use boners in same way.

Tongue Twisters on cards. Same idea. See if you can say them three times, fast, to your neighbor.

Dividing into Groups. Often there will be 50 people seated at one long table. Candles may be used for dividers. Those between candles constitute group, or those between candle and end of table. Then these small groups can be asked to "make up something."

Doing a Skit, or Singing Commercial. These can be fun, if brief. (If the group is very large, table can do its skit for neighboring table and then neighboring table reciprocates.) Singing commercials for causes of group, or for St. Valentine, for Uncle Sam, or for Witches' Brew or Santa Claus can be composed and rendered. This brings group participations.

Puppeteers. After table has been cleared (if there is time) furnish each table with paper sacks, paper, paste, paints, crayons, and let them make puppets and put on little puppet show, either for entire group or for neighboring table. (In latter case, several presentations may be going at same time.)

Art Work. After tables are cleared, bring out some fun materials for those sitting there, such as piling straws, modeling clay, crayolas. Have brief show after meal is over, showing results of this creative activity.

Performances. Members of group who have rehearsed in advance present talent, skits and stunts, singing commercials, magic show, and the like.

Honoring. Table presents natural grouping for honoring member of group (or several) who have achieved, served, or have been recognized professionally, in unusual ways. Same is true of retiring from organization. Make it sincere, to the point, but don't let it get sloppy and maudlin. Sing "Jolly Good Fellow" to retiree, give him silly gift before big one. Try to make him feel that he is welcome to come back—that this is not good-bye forever.

Revolving Banquet. Here is preplanned system for making sociability. At given signal, all those who have roses on their place cards, pick up water and napkin, and move to next position to their right, bearing rose place card. This idea is carried out twice more (adding coffee cup to moving process), with tulip place card people moving second time, and lily of valley place card people moving last time. Same could be done with numbers or other identification.

PART II

Materials For Fun

Group Starters

Anyone in charge of a recreational event is concerned at the outset that it get off to a good start. The chief desire is that a group spirit of friendliness and fellowship develop as quickly as possible. The leader therefore sizes up the situation and introduces activities accordingly, adapting as necessary.

TYPES OF ACTIVITIES

There are at least three types of activities that are useful with groups: absorbers, group starters, and warm-ups.

1. **Absorbers**. When people arrive for an event over as much as a thirty-minute period, this kind of activity is one which can take on new people as they come so that they can join in with a minimum of effort. Such activities are: group singing, simple equipment games, telling or reading humorous material, trying physical feats, easy folk games, mixers, entertaining stunts, or learning and practicing new dance steps.
2. **Group Starters**. These are activities which begin to get the group spirit moving the instant they are used. They may be similar to the first type, but they are more group oriented. Preparatory activities for guests to take part in an arrival (like making name tags, decorating a table, helping present a puppet show, or making a hat or costume to be worn later in the party) are really group starters because they give the participant a sense of responsibility for the success of the event.
3. **Warm Ups**. These are group starters, too, but these activities assume that most of the guests are present and that now the leader needs to begin an activity which fosters an enthusiastic group spirit. Group singing or an informal activity like trying to identify the label that is one's own back by asking questions of many people or identifying baby pictures of those who are present make the individuals present more group conscious. Warm Ups may be nonsensical and may involve exercisers, noise making, group singing, gags, or mixers and simple activities.

To get a group started informally, a leader needs to keep in mind possible activities around which a group can be built. For instance, groups anywhere outdoors could be tossing a Frisbee around and this activity can catch the interest and attention of others and draw them to the fun.

Humorous material should not be underestimated for its value in molding a group—gags, jokes, boners, short stories read aloud, or other bits of fun with which people have been entertaining each other for centuries.

In addition to the types of activities mentioned, there are a number of specific one-person and group stunts which foster a group spirit. These are designed to be directed by a leader with a number of kinds of audience participation:

Tongue Twisters
Fun with Noises
Fun with Motions

Stretchers
Fun with Your Neighbors
Gags and Group Responses
Feats and Puzzles

TONGUE TWISTERS

Some tongue twisters really do not twist the tongue but follow a pattern of alliteration, beginning every word with the same letter, which is not particularly hard to pronounce. Tongue twisters are said three times very fast; to be difficult, the words do not have to be long.

1. Bisquick, kiss quick!
2. She sells sea shells by the seashore.
3. Six slippery, sliding snakes.
4. Fat friars fanning flames.
5. Great gilt gig whip.
6. Jack Jackson Zachary.
7. The judge jugged Judd.
8. This'll sift the thistle sifter.
9. Three terrible thieves.
10. Flatfish fleets flee fast.
11. The zither sizzed.
12. Listless lisping lacks luster.
13. The bank book blew back.
14. The girl with the green, gray geese.
15. Tim, the thin twin tinsmith.

If you wish to make up your own Tongue Twisters, these represent hard combinations to say:

Si, Sa, Se, Si, So, Su
Six, Sick
Z, J
Jud, Jug
Strong Th followed by S, T, or Tl
Sw, Sm

Ch, Cl
Tw, Ta, Te, Ti, To, Tu
Pl, Pa, Pe, PI, PO, Pu
Bl, Br
Gr, Ga, Ge, Gi, Go, Gu

How To Use Tongue Twisters

Just for fun, pass out slips with twisters on the back and see if one person can say them to another person and rotate each time to another group member. Another method is to divide into groups and have each group repeat a twister together; determine the best response. Or, run a contest among individuals chosen from each group and coached by the group to see who is best at the twisters.

FUN WITH NOISES

Big Sneeze. Group one says HISH. Group two says HASH. Group three says HOSH. Next, each group adds "ee" to the end of its word, in order. Then they say them all together in a tremendous sneeze—to which the proper answer of the leader is, "Gesundheit!"

Football. Divide the participants into two teams and name each, perhaps Lions and Tigers. Leader stands where all can see, with hands extended in front, a little lower than shoulder high, palms down. The left hand makes signals for the Tigers and the right for Lions. On a blast from a whistle, the game begins; each team starts yelling and the leader marks their progress. If Tigers are louder than Lions, the hand indicating that group goes up and the Lion hand lowers. Tigers continue yelling, but Lions must shift to booing. If Lion booing is loud enough, it can bring the balance back and tip it over so that they are louder than the Tigers; in this case, Lions now yell and cheer, and Tigers boo. If the leader feels that enough noise has been made by one side to make a touchdown, both hands are raised high in the air and a long blast on the whistle ends the game. (Actually, it is difficult to tell who is yelling louder, but this is a wonderful way to warm up a group.)

Frog Pond. Without telling the guests why, ask a third of the group (high voices) to say in falsetto "Tomatoes, tomatoes, tomatoes, tomatoes." Ask another third (middle voices) to say more slowly, "Potatoes, potatoes, potatoes, potatoes." Ask the rest of the group (low voices) to say very slowly: "Friied bacon! Friiied bacon! Friiiiied bacon!"

Hooray! System is announced. If the right hand is raised, the group is to respond "Hooray!". If the left hand is raised, the group applauds violently. If both hands are raised, the group does both. Practice once. The leader then makes a few statements, for instance: "The officers have just voted a $10 increase in dues." (Horray!) "There will be no desert tonight." (Applause!) "Knowing how much you will enjoy it, the speaker is going to talk for two and a half hours." (Horray and applause!)

Steam Engine in the Roundhouse (uses five groups to make the noises). Once there was a little old engine in the roundhouse with the steam up. It was almost time to go to the station; it was on the track steaming:

Group 1 "COF-fee, COF-fee, COF-fee."
The engineer pulled back the throttle a little, and it sounded like:

Group 2 "Fissssh and chips, fissssh and chips, fissssh and chips."
Soon it was going faster:

Group 3 "Meat and carrots, meat and carrots, meat and carrots."
By now it was really highballing down the track, and it said:

Group 4 "Cheese and crackers, cheese and crackers, cheese and crackers"
Then the engineer pulled on the whistle cord:

Group 5 "Zoop! Zooooop!"

FUN WITH MOTIONS

Change Seats. The leader announces that, ten seconds after a given signal to start, each person will change to a new seat. For instance, those born in January, February, and

March are to move to the far left; April, May, and June to left center; July, August, September to right center; and the rest to the right. After the move is made, get acquainted with your neighbor. ''Ready? Go!''

Clap Hello. Have everyone extend both hands directly to the front, palms facing in. Clap hands four times, slap thighs four times, stamp floor four times, alternating from left to right foot, twice on each foot. Repeat twice more, at the end saying a good, loud ''Hello''.

Clap Rhythm. To greet or honor someone, clap rhythm can be used:

1-2-3-4, 1-2, 1-2, 1-2-3-4, 1-2, 1-2, 1-2-3-4, 1-2-3-4, 1

Commas indicate pauses and the number one at the last should be one big ending clap. If anyone has missed the rhythm, he starts over. A cowboy version is to do (during the last two sets of 4 counts) a long whoop as group is clapping 1-2-3-4, and a tremendous whoop at the end.

Pat Head, Rub Stomach. Have each individual pat his head with one hand and rub his stomach with the other, then reverse hands. (The second is much harder.)

Row Sway. With a group seated side by side in rows, ask each person to cross hands in front, take the hand of neighbor on the right and left. A slight pull by everyone with their right hands causes the entire row to sway; the same with the left. Try it with one row starting to the right, with the next row behind going to the left. Each person is to get acquainted with the new people on each side.

STRETCHERS

Exercises. Have the group stand and follow the directions of this exercise:

> Hands on your hips, hands on your knees,
> Put them behind you, if you please!
> Touch your shoulders, touch your nose,
> Touch your ears, touch your toes.
>
> Raise your hands high in the air,
> At your sides, on your hair.
> Raise your hands high as before
> While you clap, ''One, two, three, four.''
>
> My hands upon my head I place,
> On my shoulders, on my face,
> Then I raise them up on high
> Make my fingers quickly fly.
>
> Put them out in front of me,
> And gently clap them ''One, two, three.''

Let's Get Acquainted. The leader instructs the group to stand up and get acquainted by having each shout his name as loudly as possible. (He waits for them to do it.) Shouts "Louder." (They do it again.) Shouts "I couldn't hear you!" (They do it again). Great to loosen up a group as a break after a long session.

Correlation Exercises

1. Have the group try grasping the nose with the right hand and right ear with left hand. Then reverse to grasping nose with left hand and right ear with right hand. Continue changing with increasing speed.
2. Make a circle with the right arm; at the same time, make a figure eight with the right foot.
3. Starting with the arms at the wides, raise the right hand shoulder high, then the left hand. Now raise the right hand above the head, then the left hand. Move the hands back down in the same manner. Try this several times.

Birds Fly. The leader calls out the names of birds or animals. If the creature flies, the group is supposed to make flying motions with the hands. If the creature does not fly, hands remain still. On "ducks fly", all would flap hands; on "horses fly", hands would remain still.

Going with the Winds. As the leader makes up a sketchy story about a traveler and mentions the names of winds, people face that direction and do proper wind motion. South wind: gentle waving motions. East wind: stronger motions. North wind: violent motions and strong "ooooing" sound. West wind: swing arms around freely. Tornado: turn around violently in place.

Obey and Omit. Much like the preceding one. Direction is given first, for instance: "Nod your heads. "Ooooooo-bey." (All nod heads.) If "Ooooooo-mit" is the word spoken after the command, instead of "Ooooooo-bey", the direction is not followed. (Sample commands: hop on foot, clap hands, turn around, mark time, shake hands with someone.)

Simon Says. The leader calls out a command to the group; if the command is "Simon says stand up", all stand up. If only the command "Stand up" is given, they are to remain still. Each keeps his own score to see who gets through with the fewest mistakes.

Three Relays (for group in auditorium)

Hand Squeeze. Everyone reaches sideward to grasp a hand of each person on the left and right. On signal, one person at the end of each row at the extreme right squeezes the hand of the person next to him. This is passed on from person to person until it reaches the extreme left, then the squeeze is returned in the same way until it reaches the original starter.

Shoulder Pinch. Hands are on the shoulders or around waists of persons to the left and right. A pinch, or squeeze, is passed from left to right down the row and returned.

Back Slap. Everyone stands with faces right. A person at the rear of the line slaps the person in front of him on the back. This slap is passed up line to the front, then everyone turns around and the slap goes back in the other direction. No one slaps until he has been slapped.

Chorus. Everyone extends the hands forward in front with palms turned inward. On signal, everyone raises his right arm up over the head of the person on his right and places his hand on the shoulder of that person. On a second signal, everyone does the same with the left arm over the head of the person at his left. On the third signal, everyone squeezes! (When the right arm is placed on the shoulder, everyone yells ''Hip''; when the left arm is placed on the shoulder, everyone yells ''Hip'' again; when everyone squeezes, all yell ''Hooray!)

Clap to Rhythm. For an exerciser, ask the group to stand and clap to the rhythm of a song, like ''Coming Round the Mountain'' or ''Dixie'' or ''Yankee Doodle''. Or tramp out the rhythm, marching in place.

I Went to Paris. The leader says: ''I went to Paris and bought a pair of shoes (shuffle feet), a pair of gloves (open and close right fist), an umbrella (open and close left fist), a hat (nod head), a pair of glasses (blink eyelids), and a set of false teeth (open and close mouth). Each person must keep doing each motion started, add each new motion and continue all until the end.

Orchestra. While singing a familiar song, the leader began to play a violin in pantomime. The rest of the guests are divided into groups, each assigned one instrument. Everybody plays his assigned instrument until the leader shifts to his particular instrument. Then those playing the instrument which the leader shifted to must play the violin. Fun is in the quick shifts!

Fancy Handshakes. (Group standing.) Leader suggests that he is going to teach some special handshakes so that the participants may greet their neighbors. Turn to the neighbor and shake hands:

1. Pump Handle Style—Pump up and down in an exaggerated manner.
2. Fisherman's Style. Take another person's hand, let hands wiggle backward and forward on a push-pull basis.
3. Model T Ford—Hold hand as if it were a crank handle and swing for everyone to shake hands with a near neighbor, on the left and then on the right. Then he asks everyone to turn around and shake hands with the person immediately behind. (If all follow the instructions, there is no one there to shake hands with, of course!)
4. Paul Bunyan Style—Each person starts shaking hands in the usual manner, but grasps the thumb of the hand he is using to shake with his free hand, and both saw away. Both yell ''Timber'' when the tree is down.
5. Automatic Transmission Style. Hands just lie in each other without grip. (No clutch!)
6. Milkmaid Style. One of the two interlaces fingers of both his hands, thumbs pointing up. Turn this combination upside down, exposing thumbs to be milked; the other person, hangs on and ''milks''.

FUN WITH YOUR NEIGHBOR

Face the person next to you and do one or two of these stunts.

Fingers Up. Hold up fists at each other. On a signal from the leader (one, two, three, GO!), each will hold up as many fingers as he wishes. The one who calls out the first correct total of elevated fingers on all four hands gets one point. Play about five times. Make 'em Yawn. Decide which will try first. Then that person keeps yawning until he makes the neighbor yawn. Reverse it. Make 'em Laugh. Same as above, except that one tries to make your neighbor laugh.

Opposites. Decide which is to be the person, which the mirror. Person then faces mirror and the mirror must reflect what the person does; then shift roles.

GAGS AND GROUP RESPONSES

Candy Store. The leader gives instructions for playing candy store. He asks that one person take a long string and hold on and then adds others until there is a long line of people holding onto the string. Then, the leader explains that this is a candy store because there are some suckers on the line!

Facial Stretcher. Give a large rubber band to each person taking part. Each puts it over his head and around his neck, with the band starting from the tip of his nose. The object is to see who can get his band down over the mouth and chin and onto the neck by using face muscles only.

How Many Birthdays You've Had. The leader says to an individual: "I can tell you how many birthdays you've had. If I can, will you get me a drink?" When he agrees, you indicate that he's had one birthday, and you're not sure how many anniversaries he's had since then.

Mind Reading. Offer to read the minds of any persons in the entire group. Ask them if they will give you a dime if you can do it. (Keep trying until someone consents.) Concentrate! Then announce to the person that you have read his mind. He thinks you're not going to get that dime!

Plane Landing. This is a stunt which requires two loud voices (Pilot and Control Tower) from different sides of the room with the people out of sight. From the Pilot's side of the room, a third person (also out of sight) makes the sound of airplane engines. The group leader says; "I think I hear a plane overhead."

> *PILOT* (yelling loudly): "Pilot to control tower, pilot to control tower—I'm coming in. Give me landing instructions!"
> *CONTROL TOWER* (in loud monotone as if through a microphone): "Control tower to pilot, control tower to pilot—why are you yelling so loud?"
> *PILOT*: "Pilot to control tower, pilot to control tower—I haven't got a radio!"

Scotsman's Money. Bend the middle fingers of both hands down into the palms, placing the knuckles together to represent the roof. All other fingers are raised, with corresponding finger tips of both hands touching; a coin is placed between the tips of the ring fingers. "You can separate the Frenchman (little fingers), the German (thumbs), the American (forefingers), but you can't separate the Scotsman (ring fingers) from his money without raising the roof!"

Sight Tester. The leader indicates he is going to test the sight of audience. He instructs all to fold hands in their laps and asks if the left thumb is on top and then asks if the right thumb is. He instructs all to concentrate on the top thumb. Keep concentrating, and slowly close their eyes. He then asks if they are closed and shut tight. His final statement: Dark, isn't it?

Spring. For this stunt, gather to the front of the group some people to be trees, birds, and babbling brooks. Then ask for a volunteer to be the most important part, the hero. When he comes to the front, have him run among the trees. "Maybe the rest of you wonder how we know it is spring; that's easy, because the sap is running through the trees!"

Who's Boss? Fold your hands together in your lap. If the left thumb is on top, you are the dominant personality who tries to run things in your own home.

Book Ends. Get two volunteers to come forward and hold books by pressing heads together with the book between them. The leader then asks if anyone can guess what this represents. (Answer: two elephants playing book ends!")

Breath Holding. Have a legitimate contest, seeing who can hold his breath the longest. After someone has almost won, have one finalist (having arranged with him in advance) take a deep breath, and hold it for a time. Then he takes a balloon from his pocket, blows breath into it and holds his breath (in the balloon) indefinitely.

Clap Out Rhythm. An individual or a group claps out the rhythm of a song for another individual or group to guess.

Coin Grab. One player has a coin in his hand, palm up. Another has his hand open, about 8 to 12 inches above the hand of the other. The object is to make the top hand swoop down and grab the coin from the other hand before it can close on the coin. (Coin holder has little chance.)

Handcuffed Couples. Tie one person's string to each wrist; the string should be about 3 to 3 1/2 inches long. Loop the other person's tring over that one before tying each end to a wrist. Both are now handcuffed to each other. The object is to get unhandcuffed without breaking the string. (To get loose, put the center of one of the strings between the wrist and loop of the partner. They are still tied but not looped to each other.)

Human Checkers. Six players are arranged on seven chairs, three girls and three boys, as shown:

GGGOBBB
1 2 3   4 5 6

The object is to get them reversed on opposite sides of the vacant chair by moves and jumps in the same order. Solution: G3 moves right. B4 jumps her. B5 moves left. G3 jumps R. G2 jumps B4. G1 moves right. B4 jumps G1. B5 jumps G2. B6 jumps G3. G3 moves right one place. G3 jumps B6. G1 jumps B5. B5 moves left one place. B6 jumps G1. G1 moves right.

Ice Talking. Holding a piece of ice in his hand, a player starts talking to his opponent. A long as he keeps talking, he may hold the ice and his time is kept with a stop watch. When he must give up talking, he hands the ice to his opponent who talks and holds the ice.

Melt the Olive. The olive (or cherry or other small object) is frozen into an ice cube. See who can melt the cube with his hands first (Using fingers to release the olive is not allowed.)

Six-Zero. Can you make a figure six in the air with your finger and a zero with your toe at the same time?

Thumb Rotation. Can you twirl one thumb clockwise and one counterclockwise at the same time?

Whose Flag? An international game is to line up flags of a number of nations for people to guess.

Touch Your Wrist. Can you press your hand forward and make your finger tip touch your wrist?

Humor

5

The good recreation leader differentiates, of course, between humor and wit, and so he uses only that material which injures no one's feelings. In other words, humor laughs *with* people and is kindly; wit laughs *at* people and is unsportsmanlike. Such types of entertainment as ridicule, cynicism, sarcasm, fun at others' expense do not build group spirit. But there are many occasions when humor may be appropriately employed to lighten the atmosphere either briefly, as in conundrums and smart sayings, verbal gags, daffynitions, and boners, or at greater length as in amusing stories based on an absurd situation, or a play on words, incongruities of time, parodies, or spoonerisms. Samples of all these types of humor are found in this chapter.

WHEN TO USE HUMOR

There are many recreational uses for humor, for the true spirit of good humor is that of fun and laughter. One leader says that humor is for the lazy man's kit, since it takes so few muscles to smile or laugh!

1. Use humor just for fun as you talk to groups or one on one.
2. Speakers, toastmasters, masters of ceremonies find humor useful for relaxing a group or driving home a point.
3. Use on signs for trees or walls of a camp or institutional building or on a home bulletin board, especially pointed jokes, daffynitions, or boners.
4. Make stand-up cards for the meal or banquet table, with a bit of humor on each. Have people read theirs to each other. Write a joke or a quip on the back of a place card; ask people to read theirs as a conversation starter.
5. Tell or read humorous material to fill in small gaps in programs. (Simply read one bit at a time, giving time for it to soak in and for the group to laugh.) Boners or short stories are especially good, but smart sayings or gags bring their fun, too.
6. Related jokes and smart sayings may be put together in combination to make skits, especially conversation between two persons. Many short skits are actually elaborated jokes.
7. In high school and college gatherings, especially freshman affairs, these can be used as conversation starters. To get partners, give boys the first halves of jokes, girls the second halves (the joke slips have been cut in two). To find a partner, find the other half of your joke!

CONUNDRUMS
(Time: 1 to 10 minutes)

Read these conundrums aloud to groups. If they can't answer, give the answer:

1. Figure this out. A man said, "How's your dog?" The other said, "I did."
   (He understood it as "house your dog.")
2. What is bought by the yard, but worn by the foot? (A rug.)
3. How can you carry water in a sieve? (Freeze it.)
4. What is the difference between a Northern Eskimo and a Southern Eskimo?
   (A Northern Eskimo says, "Glub-glub," but a Southern one says, "Glub-glub, you-all.")
5. Why do hens lay eggs only in the daytime? (Because at night they become
   roosters.)
6. What is a go-getter? (A man out of gas, two miles from a filling station.)
7. What is a sheep after he is six years old? (Seven years old.)
8. Explain this situation: A train is on the track in Norway, with a Norwegian
   engineer, headed toward Sweden. A Swedish train is on the same track, with
   an intoxicated engineer, headed toward Norway. They both continue to their
   destinations, running on the same track. Why is there no wreck? (Because
   Norse is Norse, and Souse is Souse, and never the twain shall meet.)
9. But what if they should meet? (Twain weck.)
10. "Did you ever hear the story about the little red wagon?" "How does it go?"
11. "Have you time for a couple of dillies?" (you ask the group).
    "Sure," is the usual reply.
    "Okay, then. Dilly, dilly!"
12. Why was the little strawberry worried? (Because his mom and pop were in a
    jam.)
13. What is a good thing to lose? (A bad reputation.)
14. What turns green in the spring? (Christmas jewelry.)
15. How is racing a horse like eating an ice cream cone? (The more you lick each
    one the faster it goes.)
16. Can you add three 9's and make 10? (9 and 9/9.)
17. This is a sign in an English hotel. Can you figure it out? 'Heresto pands pen
    dasoci al hou rinhar mlessmirt ha nd funlet friends hipre ign be just an dk
    indan devil sp eakof no ne." (Here stop and spend a social hour in harmless
    mirth and fun, let friendship reign, be just and kind, and evil speak of none.)
18. Did you ever see a:
    barn dance, horse fly, board walk, milk pail, house fly, lip stick, bottle neck,
    banana split . . . (Encourage group to fill in some more.)
19. What is a question that to answer truthfully, you cannot answer no? (What
    does y-e-s spell?)
20. Question that cannot be answered truthfully with "yes." (Are you asleep?)
21. A question to which you cannot answer "yes" or "no" without incriminating
    yourself. ('Have you stopped mistreating your family?')
22. In a luggage shop a man priced some luggage. "This size for $20; this size for
    $10." The man said, "So do I." (Key: this sighs for $20!)

SMART SAYINGS
(Time: 1 to 10 minutes)

I said to the hostess on the plane, "How about stepping out?" She answered, "All
right," and went to the side door, saying, "This way out."

One swallow does not make a swimmer.

The reason a dog has so many friends is that he wags his tail instead of his tongue.

"You look like a million. By the way, how old *are* you?"

Did you hear about the Texan who got engaged and gave his girl a diamond—mine?

Everybody wears a bathing suit in Atlantic City, but it's mostly a matter of form.

"Yes, ma'am, we ship out our fertilizer to the small towns to make them grow."

Men fall in love with women who ask questions they can answer!

"Do big ships like this sink very often, captain?"
"No, only once."

VERBAL GAGS
(Time: 1 to 10 minutes)

Sometimes it's the verbal gag with a punch line that will unbend a stiff moment and pull the group together in a hearty laugh.

> Have you ever heard these three special sneezes? Try them:
> The suspicious sneeze—Whoisshe?
> The chocolate sneeze—Hershey
> The hayfever toast—Here's looking atchoooo!

The train stopped with a jerk. (The jerk got off and the train went on.)

A thick-haired gent was bothering a bald one with remarks. The bald head replied, "The deader the wood, the longer the moss."

Sharp, and the world sharps with you; flat, and you flat alone! (RUSSELL AMES COOK)

"What do you do for exercise?"
"Oh, I read mysteries and let my flesh crawl."

Did you hear of the fellow who holds the new record for staying under water? Twenty-one minutes! (Services tomorrow at 2:00.)

"What are you taking for your dyspepsia?"
"I don't know—make me an offer!"

"Guess I'll hit the hay," said the farmer, as he slid off the barn.

Say, have you heard about the new men's perfume direct from Texas? It's called Corral No. 5.

DAFFYNITIONS
(Time: 1 to 10 minutes)

This form of humor, usually based on the pun or sound of words, is generally popular in those circles in which people like to play with words.

CYNIC. Article of kitchen equipment.
DECEIT. The place you sit.
ARREARS. What we listen with.
REPARTEE. An insult with its tuxedo on.
DIETING. Triumph of the mind over platter.
BACTERIA. The rear entrance of a cafeteria.
TRUE GENTLEMAN. When your husband holds open the door while you carry in the groceries.
BIGAMIST. A man who has made the same mistake twice.
DIVINE. What grapes grow on.
SADDLE. A big town in the State of Washington.
MINER. One who can make a living by going into the hole.
PILLAGE. What a doctor makes his living from.
INDISCREET. Where children should not play after school.
GRUDGE. Place to keep your auto.
ALARM CLOCK. Device for waking a childless household.
BATHING SUIT. Garment to help the girls outstrip one another on the beach.
PESSIMIST. One who looks through morose-colored glasses.
COOKBOOK. A volume with many stirring chapters.
GRAND JURY. Anyone that acquits you.
CEREAL. The stuff that heroes are made of.
DUCK. A chicken in snowshoes.
SKELETON. Bones with the people scraped off.
INSULATE. What you have to explain for getting.
HOSPITALITY. The art of making somebody feel at home when you wish they were.
FAME. What you get by dying at the right time.
PERPETUAL MOTION. Cow drinking her own milk.
HUG. Roundabout expression of affection.
CHILDISH GAME. One at which your wife beats you.
YARN. To open your mouth wide when sleepy.
SALT. The stuff that makes potatoes taste bad when you boil 'em and don't put any in.
BACHELOR. A fellow whose only ties are those that need cleaning.
CHIVALRY. The attitude of a man toward somebody else's wife.
SARONG. A dish towel gone high society.
ETIQUETTE. Knowing which hand to use when you put your napkin in your collar.
DARK AGES. Knight time.
GENIUS. The will to turn on your thoughts instead of TV.
SMALL TOWN. Where you can chat on the phone even when you get a wrong number.
BOSS. The one who gets to the office early when you're late.
OLD AGE. When it takes you longer to get over a good time than have it.
REINDEER. A horse with a TV antenna.
INTOXICATION. When you feel sophisticated but can't pronounce it.

TANGERINE. A loose-leaf orange.

TRANSPARENTS. Those that anybody can see through.

MIDDLE AGE. When the doctor stops calling you "old girl," and starts referring to you as "young lady."

OPERA. The only place where a man, stabbed in the back, sings instead of dying.

PERSONALITY. The ability to get along on banana oil instead of elbow grease.

MIDDLE AGE. When you look back to see that the mountain you've been climbing is only a molehill. (Or, when you can't eat your cake and have It too.)

SMALL TOWN. Where everybody knows everybody else's business and reads the papers only to see if they got caught at it.

BONERS
(Time: 1 to 10 minutes)

God's Own Country is Heaven.

A juvenile is what King Saul threw at David when he was playing the harp to him.

A man is an animal split halfway up and walks on the split end.

An octupus is a person who hopes for the best.

Acrimony, sometimes called holy, is another name for marriage.

A compliment is when you say something to another which he and we know is not true.

A monologue is a conversation between two people, such as husband and wife.

An optimist is a man who looks after your eyes, a pessimist looks after your feet.

A Senator is half horse and half man.

SOS is a musical term meaning same only softer.

"Laissez-faire" meant "Let the farmers pay the taxes."

Robinhood is a word like boyhood or girlhood, it means to feel like a robin and hop around.

A sirloin is the only article of clothing worn by Gandhi, the leader of India.

A spectre is a man who doesn't believe in things like Santa Claus.

An incinerator is a person who hints bad things instead of coming right out and telling you.

Maneuver is what they put on grass. We have maneuver on our lawn.

Queen Victoria was the only queen who sat on a thorn for sixty-three years.

Yom Kippur was a general in the Japanese army.

The clown in *As You Like It* was named Touchdown.

The proof that the witches in *Macbeth* were supernatural is that no one could eat what they cooked.

Some instruments used in an orchestra are: viles, cellars, trumpets, hornets, baboons, old boys, and bubble bases.

Write a sentence showing clearly the meaning of "posterity."

He had a cat, but nothing else lived on his posterity.

The man looked as if he had been reduced to posterity.

Henry paid the fare because of his posterity.

By his clothes he seemed a person of great posterity.

The cat leaped about and then sat on its posterity.

There are three kinds of poetry—lyric, dramatic, and epidemic.

The theme of this poem is that Longfellow shot an arrow into the air, and many years afterward he found it in the heart of a friend.

A poetic license is a license you get from the Post Office to keep poets. You get one also if you want to keep a dog. It costs two dollars and you call it a dog license.

First to thine own self be true,

Thou can'st then be false to any man.

Degrees of comparison of "Bad":

Bad: very sick: dead.

General Braddock was killed in the French and Indian war, he had three horses shot under him and a fourth went through his clothes.

Abraham Lincoln wrote the Gettysburg Address while traveling from Washington to Gettysburg on the back of an envelope.

Queen Elizabeth was a very wise, good queen, and so she never married.

The difference between a king and a president is that a king is the son of his father, but a president isn't.

Blockheads were the part cause of the War of 1812.

Martin Luther died a horrible death. He was excommunicated by a bull.

Watchword of the French Revolution: Liberty, Equality, and Maternity.

The Duck of Wellington won a big battle and when he finished he had one arm and one eye and he looked through the telescope with his blind eye and said it was all right and that is how he won the battle.

Horace Greeley was the worst defeated candidate ever elected.

The Spartan mother used to say to her son, "Return with your shield or pawn it."

The seats of Senators shall be vaccinated every six years.

The pilgrims landed at Plymouth Rock. They were greeted by the Indians who came running down the hill rolling their war hoops before them.

In Pittsburgh they manufacture iron, and steal.

The alimentary canal is located in the northern part of Indiana.

Where is the greater part of Europe?

In New York.

Manhattan Island was bought from the Indians for about $24 and now I don't suppose you could buy it for $500.

The original tribes of Central America were the Aztecs, the Cults, and the Morons.

An Indian reservation consists of a mile of land for every five square Indians.

Jacob, son of Isaac, stole his brother's birth mark.

Water is composed of two gins, Oxygin and Hydrogin. Oxygin is pure gin, Hydrogin is gin and water.

The difference between air and water is that air can be made wetter, but water cannot.

When you breathe you inspire. When you do not breathe you expire.

Why do we not raise the silk worm in the United States?

We get our silk from the rayon. He is a larger animal and gives more silk.

A good milk cow can be told by her rudder.

Sea water has the formula CH_2O.

Explain the effect of heat and cold and give an illustration.

Heat expands: in the summer the days are long.

Cold contracts: in the winter the days are short.

What is an individual?

An individual is a piece of people.

Inertia is when you go on after you stop and when you stop after you start.

Buddha lived a normal life with a wife and family, and when he was thirty, left home in search of happiness.

Who were the Albigenses and where did they live?

I don't know who they were nor where they lived, but whoever they were and wherever they lived, I wish them a Merry Christmas.

What are the two characteristic differences of the anatomy of the infant and the adult?

The infant's anatomy is straight and narrow. The adult's is protruding and wider.

The food goes down the food pipe and the Effougis shushes it off from going down the wind pipe.

To stop blood from flowing from a wound in the leg, wrap the leg around the body above the heart.

Often when people are drowned you can revise them by punching in their sides but not too hard. This is called resurrection.

They say music hath charms to soothe the savage beast, but I never noticed it had any effect on me.

Some men came to Jesus with a penny and he asked them, "Whose subscription is this?"

When my grandma lived in Germany she found a nest of snake's egges and she went there and hatched them. She hatched them with a hatchet.

When you want to kill a hog, you stab him in the aqueduct.

At the X mine, after sinking a shaft one hundred feet, they finally struck bed-pan.

Everybody should not try to do everything but should do one thing well. For instance cows can always give milk, but hens cannot do this. They prefer to lay eggs.

THE LEGEND OF THE BLUE GNUS
(Time: 5 minutes)

Once upon a time, in the land of Zoos lived a pair of bright blue gnus. One was a cute girl gnu named Sue and the other was a boy, and his name was Hugh. Every day when they would meet, they would say something like this: "Yoo hoo, Hugh, you blue gnu you!" or "Yoo hoo, Sue, you cute gnu, you!"

Yes, Hugh loved Sue, and Sue loved Hugh, and they carried on like lovers do. They would get in the corner (just the two) and oh, how they would bill and coo! Hugh said to Sue one day, "I need yer. Let's go out and find the preacher!"

Well, they found the preacher, and had a wedding. He said, "Do you, Sue Gnu, love Hugh Gnu?" She replied, "Yes, of course I do." Hugh took the ring hidden in his hose, and put it in his new bride's nose. The wedding feast went on for hours, with all the guests eating up all the flowers. Oh, the gnuspapers were full of it the next day!

After the honeymoon Hugh went to work for the gnuspaper. Every day when he went to work Sue would smile at him and smirk, "Goodbye, Hugh, you blue gnu you." And of course he'd say, "Good-bye, Sue. Good-bye to you, you cute gnu, you!" Then he'd give her a great big kiss every day, he'd never miss.

Hugh had a very interesting job. At his work he worked hard every day, and to get his pay, he must have the cross-word puzzles call for "a three-lettered animal." Of course, this meant "gnu." Since three-lettered spaces are hard to fill, Hugh would usually fill the bill!

Back at home Hugh and Sue were happy gnus. "There is just one thing," Hugh often said, day by day since they were wed, "One thing that our love nest lacks. We need the patter of little feet! The love of a child just can't be beat. We need the laughter of a tiny blue gnu!" To that Sue said, "A little gnu or two."

Then an idea came to Hugh. "I know just what we can do! Let's adopt a little blue gnu!"

"You are right," said Sue, "let's glance at the gnuspaper and see if there's a chance!"

Both took the paper and they looked and looked, but all orphan gnus just seemed to be booked. Nobody knew a tiny little gnu who wanted to be adopted by some gnus—do you?

Sue and Hugh became discouraged. Gradually the two began to fuss. (Gnus make noise, but of course they don't cuss.) Hugh would say, "Foo to you, Sue! Foo-foo to you, you blue gnu you!"

Poor little Sue would cry, "Boo-hoo! Poo-poo to you, you old blue gnu, you!"

Yes, their home was nice and neat, but it needed the patter of little feet. They wanted the laughter of a little blue gnu to brighten their present and their later years, too.

The problem soon took its toll at Hugh's work. It bothered him so when he went to work that, though he worked as hard as a Turk, there came a time (he just couldn't see how) when for three-lettered animals in the puzzles they used the term, "a cow." This, of course, made Hugh Gnu sad, and it also made him very mad.

He came home to his little place one night in a nasty mood, just spoiling for a fight. He yanked the door open and he stalked right in, making lots of noise as he went in. But then he took one look at Sue and saw in her eyes a light that was new. Gone was the frown from Sue's pretty brow. She looked so sweet and peaceful now. A happy smile beamed on her face, and as she moved there was a new kind of grace.

"Sue," was all that Hugh could say, "What has made you look this way?"

She came over close, and he could see that she differed from the way she used to be.

"Sh-h-h-h-h!" was all Sue said to Hugh. "Darling . . . I have gnus for you!"

IT ALL STARTED WITH EUROPA

Europe at the Beginning

The beginnings of Europe are shrouded in impenetrable myths. According to one of these, Europe was named after Europa, a girl who rode around on a bull named Jupiter. The fact that Jupiter was actually not a bull but a god . . . gives us some indication of the uncertainty of those early days. All Europa knew was that it was transportation.

Except for lending her name, Europa had little to do with Western civilization. Some scholars, however, detect her influence on Far Western culture, notably the custom of riding the bull at rodeos and slinging it at dude ranches and Bar-B-Q's.

Europe is also called the Old Country, the Old World, and Where My People Came From. People who live in Europe are called Europeans until they emigrate to America, where they are called Foreigners.

GEOGRAPHY AND CLIMATE

Europe, like the rest of the Earth, was originally too hot to handle. It had no sooner cooled off than it was covered by ice as far as the eye could see, and even farther. The northernmost region was populated by Ice Men who carried ice picks and traveled in ice packs. It was generally agreed that what Europe needed was a good thaw, but while everybody talked about it, nobody did anything. Waiting for the ice to retreat to the north, a few inches a year, the Europeans grew increasingly impatient. They were eager to discover places like Norway and Sweden and to see their first Great Dane.

After the ice left, Europe was covered with dense forests, which first had to be cleared and later carefully preserved. The forests could hardly be seen because of the trees, and were full of fierce animals ready to spring, and fierce birds ready to chirp. Lakes, dug out by glaciers, provided our European ancestors with picturesque scenery and healthful spas. To these latter they went to take baths, which they badly needed, and to recover from the gout, an ailment which it was as much fun to get as to get over.

In those days, which were extremely B.C., England was part of Europe, and Ireland, much to the disgust of the Irish, was part of England. Owing to the absence of the English Channel, channel swimming was virtually unknown.

Europe and Africa were still connected at Gibraltar, which was of no strategic importance and therefore not held by the British. Maps were very poor, and it was hard to distinguish Asia Minor from Asia Major and Asia Proper from Asia Improper. The largest region was the Unknown World, an area not yet Ripe for Conquest and Colonialization.

Prehistoric Man

According to Darwin, the first men hung from the branches of trees by their tails. It was not until much later that they discovered ropes and began to hang each other. For some reason, our ancestors' tails got shorter and shorter, and the fun gradually went out of swinging. Whether or not men descended from the monkeys, as soon as they lost their tails they descended from trees.

The earliest Europeans were Homo Sapiens, Neanderthal, and Cro-Magnon. The latter, because of his hyphenated name, was probably British. Little is known of these original men, except that Homo Sapiens was the brightest and Cro-Magnon had a long head. Nothing favorable has ever been said about Neanderthal, although his masculinity was unquestioned. He had the hairiest chest until Ernest Hemingway.

THE STONE AGE

After the Ice Age came the Stone Age. Stones had certain advantages over ice. For instance:

1. They were warmer, especially when left in the sun.
2. They didn't melt on the way home.
3. They gave employment to stone masons and made possible the naming of Stonewall Jackson.

On the other hand, they were inferior to ice in certain respects:

1. They were no good for iced drinks.
2. They were unsatisfactory for skating on.

Fortunately, stones were plentiful. Furthermore, there was little or no depreciation, and a used stone was as good as a brand-new one. Geology was in its infancy, and rock gardening was unknown.

LIFE IN THESE EARLY TIMES

We must not suppose that Europeans of the Stone Age felt thwarted by their failure to discover bronze and iron. Whittling away thoughtfully on stones, hunting wild beasts and women, they kept busy. The more energetic of them left no stone unturned.

Let us picture the daily life of one of our ancestors. Rising early, perhaps awakened by the dripping of water from a stalactite directly overhead, he makes his toilet by untangling his hair from his eyebrows and rubbing a small stone over his well-developed incisors, being careful to use an up-and-down stroke. He has a light breakfast of roots, berries, and raw mastodon meat, completely unaware that every mouthful is bursting with vitamins.

Putting the rumpled earth back into place, he makes his bed. This is woman's work, he thinks, and is reminded of his day's chores. He must find a double-breasted animal to skin for a new suit, and a woman to be his mate.

With a quick backward glance at his cave, and making a mental note to arch the top of his doorway a little, like his neighbor's, he is off on his appointed rounds. Avoiding the brontosauruses and thesauruses, which are a bit large for his purpose, he searches out a saber-toothed tiger and removes the skin. Unless he has in mind military regalia, he also removes the saber.

The woman is a little more of a problem, but not much. Our ancestor has a poor posture, his forehead is repellent to those who prefer the intellectual type, and his teeth cry out for the attention of an orthodontist. But there is something exciting about the way he can beat a woman over the head with a club. He knows the right spot, just above the ears, and his blows have a certain manly authority about them. By mid-afternoon he has clubbed a smart-looking brunette into a swoon. Taking her silence to mean assent, he seizes her by the forelock, or anything handy, and drags her away. Whatever skin comes off along the road, he says to himself, will grow back.

As the shadows of late afternoon lengthen, our ancestor and his bride arrive home, unencumbered by rice or old shoes. He carries her over the threshold of the cave and tenderly drops her. The honeymoon is over. As soon as she regains consciousness, she assumes the wifely duties, cutting the tiger skin into long lapels and natural shoulders, preparing a supper of left-over mastodon meat, and enlarging the dugout portion of the floor to make a double bed.

Little does our ancestor think, as he nestles his head into the clod that serves as his pillow, that in a few thousand years men will be urged to return to nature. He, although he does not appreciate his good fortune, is already there.

ARTS AND CRAFTS

Paintings were usually done right on the walls of caves, to save the expense of framing. Nude portraits were popular, especially those of deer and bison. But, since this was the dawn of civilization, the light was poor, and artists were unable to do their best work. They were scornfully called Primitives by those who knew nothing about art but knew what they liked. In terms of years, if not ability, Primitives must be considered the genuine Old Masters.

As the shapes and sizes of stones improved, craftsmen made spectacular advances in such fields as wood carving, meat carving, and murder.

We owe much to prehistoric man. It does not seem likely, however, that we can ever repay him.

IT ALL STARTED WITH COLUMBUS

The Discovery of America

America was founded by Columbus in 1492. This is an easy date to remember because it rhymes with "ocean blue," which was the color of the Atlantic in those days. If he had sailed a year later the date would still be easy to remember because it would rhyme with "boundless sea."

Columbus fled to this country because of persecution by Ferdinand and Isabella, who refused to believe the world was round, even when Columbus showed them an egg. Ferdinand later became famous because he objected to bullfights and said he perferred to smell flowers if he had to smell anything. He was stung in the end by a bee.

Before Columbus reached America, which he named after a man called American Vesuvius, he cried "Ceylon! Ceylon!" because he wanted to see India, which was engraved on his heart, before he died. When he arrived, he cried again. This time he cried "Excelsior!" meaning "I have found it."

Columbus was mistaken in thinking he had reached India when actually he had not got even as far as Indiana. There is still a great deal of confusion about the East and the West. As Columbus discovered, if you go west long enough you find yourself in the east, and vice versa. The East and the West are kept apart by the Date Line, just as the North and South are kept apart by the Masons' Dixon Line. In the New World most of the eastern half of the country is called the Middle West, although it is known as the East by those who live in the Far West.

Columbus, who was as confused as anybody who has been at sea for a long time, called the first people he saw "Indians." It is not known what they called Columbus. His unfortunate error has been perpetuated through the centuries. The original Americans are still known as "Indians," while all manner of immigrants from England, Ireland, Angora, and Lichtenstein are referred to as "Americans."

Accompanied by his devoted followers, the Knights of Columbus, Columbus made several other voyages in search of India. Try as he might, however, he kept discovering America, and finally returned to Spain to die. He lived for a time in Madrid, but spent his last days in Disgrace.

A MINORITY OPINION

Some say it was not Columbus who discovered America but a man named Leaf Ericson. Leaf came from one of the Scandinavian countries with a shipload of people, all of whom were called Yon Yonson or Ole Olson or Big Swede, and went straight to Wisconsin, where he unloaded his passengers and went back for more.

On his next trip he went to Minnesota.

We know all this from some undecipherable remarks he made on a piece of stone. This stone has since become an utter rune.

FURTHER EXPLORATIONS

After Columbus proved the world was round, a great many people went around it. Marco Polo, who was one of the earlier explorers, had the misfortune to live several centuries before Columbus. Therefore, although he got around a good deal, he did not get completely around. He went far to the north, however, and is remembered for his discovery of the Polo regions.

The chief rivals in exploration were England and Spain. England had men like Cabot, who spoke only to a man named Lowell, and Sir Francis Drake, who had a singed beard and a ship, the Golden Behind.

Nor should we forget Sir Martin Fourflusher.

The struggle between England and Spain came to a climax in an epic sea battle off the Azores known as the Last Fight of the Revenge. In this decisive conflict, Sir Richard Grenville and Alfred Lord Tennyson proved conclusively that the lighter English warships could get more miles to the galleon.

England has ruled the waves ever since and has kept the sun from setting anywhere on her empire, this providing a longer working day than in other countries.

STILL FURTHER EXPLORATIONS

Other explorers included Bilbo, Cabbage de Vaca, Cortez (known as the Stout, who traveled much in realms looking for gold), and Pantsy de Lion, a thirsty old man who was looking for a drinking fountain. He never found it, but he founded Florida, to which a great many thirsty old men have gone ever since.

DER JACKASSERS UND DER ROPER

Der barnyarden insiden ben ein brownisch Jackasser mit ein shorten roper aroundergehooken der necken. Also gehooken mit das roper ben ein whitisch Jackasser.

Der brownisch Jackasser ben wanten ein haystacker on der leften und der whitischer ben wanten ein haystacker on der righten. Mit snorten under grosser grunten-groanen der Jackassers ben tuggen und strainen und pawen der earthen mitout succeeden!

Finaller der dumkopfs ben gestoppen der pullen und obertalken ein schemer. Suddener, der Jackassers iss rushen aparten pellmellen mit breaknecken speeden! Ach! Der roper ben gebroken! Der neckers also ben gebroken.

JOHANN HORNER

Der smallisch Johann Horner
Ben gesitten in das corner
Der Yuletiden strudel gestauffen.
Der thumber in-gesticken
Und out-gepullen quicken
Mit burnen und blisters gepuffen!

Der oldisch rhymer ben claimen Johann iss outgepullen ein plum mit braggen, "Ach! Ich ben ein gooten boy!" Iss ein mistooker. Iss gooten youngischers ben gesitten in das corner? Nein. Johann ben ein littlisch schtunker und der fader und mutter ben outgaben der punishen. Ich ben gethinken iss better ein backwhacken. Und mitout strudel.

THE TARE AND THE HORTOISE

Once a-time a pon, a big ray grabbit was faking a lot of mun of a tazy old lortoise for always slooving so moe-ly. "Oh, bosh!" tied the crortoise. "You just bait a wit! Why, I can fan so much ruster than you, my fine-frethered fend, that I shall inch you within a leat of your bife!'' The labbit raffed, but the sere-toise was torious. ''In that case,'' rehied the plare, inking his wye at a bander-sty, ''let's sigh it and tree!''

So they finally decided to hire a fly sox to ket the source for them and to goot off the shun to rart the stace. It was a dright, bunny say, as a big grad cowthered and there were chowed leers as the two constartents tested. Soon the hare was so har afed that he thought it was tie hime to take a right slest, so he day quietly lown on the croft gool sass and snarted to store. But the old, toe slortoise kept odding and odding plon and finally geached the roal. The croise of the nelling yowd hoke the weeping slare, and he duddenly sashed on, gossing the croal line several limits mayter.

And The Storal to This Mory Is: No matter how fast a rubbit can ran, he will never surtass a torpoise when it comes to wearing turtleswecked netters.

KELLING THE BAG

In a herten souse there lived a kye slat who just moted on dice. Every time the mice'd tie to have a good trime, the spat would coil it. So the mice decided to cold a hoart to fix it so they would know when the keeline was fumming so they could scamper safe to offty. ''If you will allow ME to be Dean for a Quay,'' said a maidy louse, ''I would suggest that there's buthing netter to warn us of the prat's a-coach than to bang a hell anound his reck.'' At first they leered chustilly, considering this a papital clan. ''However, though,'' udded anather, ''now that we're a-beed on the grell, who is the maive brouse who is going to cold the hat while we put it around the nat's keck?'' But there was bro one naive enough to kell the bat.

And The Storal to This Mory Is: A small tell binkles and a large tell bowls, but what's the mifference if you're a douse?

THE MYON AND THE LOUSE

Way back before Crossington delled the Washaware, a late big gryon was deeping peacefully in his slen, beaming of a dreef-steak, when he was awakened by a mee wouse, running fack and borth afoss his crace. Toozing his lemper, the gryon labbed the mittle louse by the nuff of the screck and was on the kerge of villing him. Moor little pouse! ''Lease, Mister Plyon,'' mide the crouse, ''if you will only get me lo, I fomise praithfully to rekind you for your payness!'' So the lierce fyon, who must have been a cub Scoy Bout in his dunger yaize, thought he would dee his daily good dude, and he set the frouse mee.

A couple of leeks waiter, this very lame syon got nangled up in a tet, and though he was Bing of the Keasts (not to be confused with Craws Bingby) no one came to answer his rellowing boars. But, chear dildren, pay is the here-off: along comes the miny little touse, and, gnawing the topes with his reeth, he frees the shyon from his lackles! ''Turn-affair is bout play!'' meaks the squouse, and with that, he hurns on his teel and heats it for bome.

And The Storal to This Mory Is: Sometimes our bubbles are trig, and sometimes our smubbles are trawl, but if we TRAD no hubbles, how would we bleckognize our ressings?

THE MUNTRY KAID AND HER PILKMAIL

Once on a dot August hay, a muvly laiden was walking slowly along a runtry code with a pilkmail balanced on her hurly kedd. (She carried it that way because the flop of her head was tat.) As she thudged along, she was trinking: ''When I mell this silk, I shall have

emuff nunny to buy deveral suzzen eggs at pryzant presses. (This was B.O. the 4 P.A.)
Out of these eggs, allowing for feveral which may not be sertil,* will come about foo
hundred and tifty chuffy young flicks. These chittle licks will grow into charge lickens
and I can marry them to carket for the Trismuss crade. Of course, in the Sooltide yeezon,
scoaltry is pairce, so by the mollowing Fay I shall be able to dry myself a brand new bess.
Now let's see . . . I think my bless shall be drew, to match the uller of my kyes, and I shall
foe to the Gair, where all the fung yellows will part me for a wantner. But to each I shall
say: 'Go feddle your pish!'"

And as she spoke thus to herself, she sauced her head tossily and off went the mail of
pilk and grilled all over the spass. Mott a whess! Mott a careless whayden!

And The Storal to This Mory Is: Don't fount your cowls before they sheeve the lell.

THE ROOGLE AND THE EASTER

Once upon a time a farmer owned a rupple of great big koosters who thought they were
nuff as tales because someone told them they were Rimmuth Plocks. So every time they
fast in the parmyard, they'd give each other the eye-vul E. They were obviously extremely
bellous jerds. So one day they pined the proper saipers, and with the jessings of Mike
Blacobs, they fought it out under the Roonsberry Queels.

For the sake of the awdies in our lady-ence, we shan't go into dorrible hee-tales, but
when the fin was fightished, one dooster lay red. The one who FUN the wight flew up to
the stoof of the raible, chuffed out his pest, and load so crowdly he could be heard wurteen
miles a-thay. He might just as well have been in the stenter of a well-lighted sage, for a
great awled beagle, who happened to by hying overfled, tabbed the royzy nooster in his
grallons and flew him to the mop of a high town-ten, where Isses Meagle made him into a
fine dicken chinner for her houd pruzzband and all their eaggy baibles.

And The Storal to This Mory Is: Fide proeth before a gawl.

THE PAG AT THE STOOL

A stursty thag went down to a quiet drool to pink. As he bent over to laist the delicious
tickwid, he was terry much vaiken with his fine anting spredlers, but when he took a
lander at his geggs, which were skin and thrawny, he experienced a feeling of heffinite
daitred.

While he stood there anting his likelers and laiting his heggs, he was attacked by a
leerce fyon. But in the face which chollowed, he soon outdistanced the Bing of the
Keasts, and he lept his keed as long as there was a lack of feeze and troaliage. But,
coming fezzantly to a prorest, he was caught by his brantlers in the antches and the gryon
labbed him in his cleeth and taws and shripped him half to reds. "Moe is wee!" stied the
crag, with his brast leth, "I laited my himbs, which might have laived my sife; but the
prorns of which I am so very howd have dooved my unprewing."

Stoor old pag! Lasty old nyon!

And The Storal to This Mory Is: What is mirth woast if often lallued veast. OR, if you
anton to have happlers, you are stobably a prag; but if the saidies per-loo you, you are
loutless a dyon.

---

*Her tuther had moaled her about the burrs and beeds.

Mixers

The purpose of mixers is to get people of a group acquainted with one another and to prevent those who already know each other well from staying in one small group during the whole period.

Name tags are an important device toward accomplishing this purpose. Clever ones can be improvised by any group. The letters must be large enough for those without their glasses to see easily.

This chapter gives at least eight categories of mixers with several suggestions in each: Handshakers, Trading or Using Objects, Gamelike Mixers, Mixers Involving Names, No-Partner Mixers, Ways of Getting Partners, Couple Mixers, Formation Mixers Using Music.

HANDSHAKERS

Lucky Shake, or Mysterious Stranger. No one knows who are distributors of prizes. Whoever happens to be tenth one to shake hands with one of them is given award.

Shake or Else. Certain types of handshakes are prescribed, and there are monitors around to check and see that all are performing. "High-society style," "Wrestler who's lost his grip," "Sore-armed baseball pitcher," "Like an old friend you haven't seen in years," and the like. At musical signal group must change each time.

Bag Shake. Each person has paper sack on his hand for handshaking.

Handshaking Down the Aisle. Have two aisles of people, down which people go, one at a time, shaking hands with right hand to persons on right, left hand to those on left, finally taking own place in line as he gets to foot of double-line.

Circle Handshake. Standing in circle, leader steps out, and with back to circle, shakes hands with person who was on his right, continuing all around circle. That person follows him as soon as leader goes to third person, and so on until all have shaken hands around circle. When each person comes back to his original place, he stops there and shakes hands with others as they come around circle. When leader gets back to his original place, all should have shaken hands with someone else, either as active handshaker or stationary one, staying in place. Finish by circling to music, swing partner (if playing by partners).

TRADING OR USING OBJECTS

Even or Odd. Each player has 10 or 15 beans. He walks up to someone and asks, "Even or odd?" (meaning number of beans he has in his closed hand). Person guesses. If he is right, he gets beans; if wrong, he pays like number of beans. See who gets most in given time.

Barter. Each player is given number of articles, such as beans, peas, small potatoes, hairpins, nuts, marbles, keys, buttons. During trading period he is to do as much trading as possible. See who has most articles at end, or place value in points on each of articles and see who has most points.

Color Barter. Same idea. Each has supply of colored squares. Trade during trading season. Colors are later assigned points, and winner is one with most points.

Numbers Mixer. Each person is given numeral big enough to be seen easily across room when pinned to him. Leader calls out certain numbers, such as 55. People organize themselves quickly to get several folk together whose number totals 55. Each gets bean for counter (or punch on his number). See who gets most. (Instead of sum, the numerals may stand in order to form given large figure, such as 13,947.)

Meal Mixer. Each person is given large, readable paper or card bearing name of food. At signal, people start out to get together complete meal of appetizer, meat, two vegetables, drink, dessert, salad.

Human Scavenger Hunt. Number of people present wear unusual clothes, mismatched sox, ring on wrong finger, and the like. Make list and have each person looking to see who is in that condition. At end see who found most. (Pencil and paper mixer.)

Who Is . . . Each person has list and writes down:

Guest with darkest hair   Guest with largest dimples
Guest with biggest feet   Guest with bluest eyes

Animal Hunt. Group is divided into several smaller ones, each with captain and animal name, such as bear, cow, horse, raccoon. Each animal is assigned color (such as red to cows) and at a signal, they go out to search for food, which consists of colored squares of paper. When player finds square, he calls with his animal noise and his captain hurries over either to claim square (if it is his) or to destroy it (if it is enemy food). At end of hunt, see which team has most squares.

Conversation System. Good for small group, especially on trip. Rule is that, having spoken to person, you cannot speak to that person again until you have spoken to everybody else.

Name Tag Rule. In conference wearing name tags, make rule that anyone caught without his tag will have to pay penalty.

Rotation. On one-hour trip for 20 people, each person was numbered and had to change seats when signal was given. This meant that everybody sat with everyone else before trip was over. Could not return to a number for second time.

Eating Buns. String rope between two trees and have hanging from it, at different heights, buns on string. Players must walk up to their buns, hands behind them, and eat them. With line jiggling, it is not too easy.

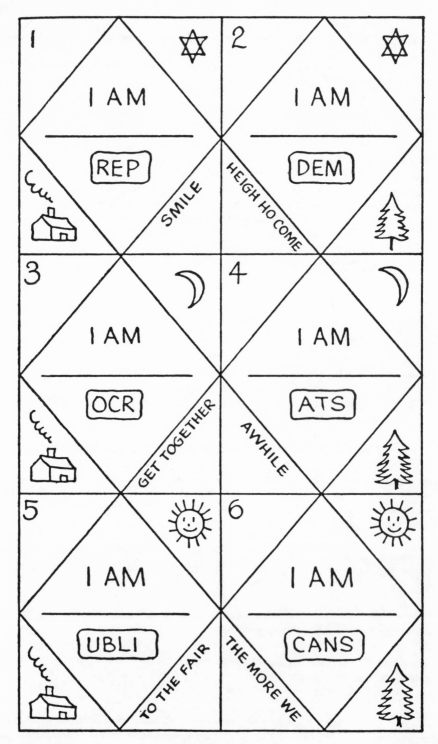

Controlled Confusion

Reminiscence. Half the group have odd numbers pinned on them, and the other half have even numbers. Instructions are distributed to one or other in slips of paper: "Find No. 14 and tell what you did on the Fourth of July." "Look up No. 7 and tell of your most interesting adventure of the year," and so on.

Controlled Confusion. Duplicate diagram shown and cut into six squares, passing them out evenly. Then get into groupings as called. Several assistants, equipped with paper punches, punch holes in paper of each player who has the winning combination—object, to see who has most punches. When players are in groups, call for each group to search among itself for answers to questions, such as these:

1. Highest number of pennies in group.
2. Largest number of Jims and Janes (or Bettys and Bobs).
3. Most people born outside of this city, or county, or state.
4. Three people with longest feet.
5. The most buffalo nickels.
6. Person with longest hair.
7. Tallest person.
8. Most wrist watches—or rings—brown shoes.
9. Most birthdays this month (be honest!)
10. Reddest sox, and so on.

Get them into groups of different sizes. Their cards will divide into two groups: houses or trees; Republicans or Democrats; also by their own last names in A to L, M to Z. (They will have written their names on their own cards.)

Three groups: Divide by sun, moon, stars, or song titles.

Four groups: By their own birth months: January to March; April to June; July to September; October to December.

Six groups: Use number in upper left-hand corner of their square.

Face to Face. Persons stand facing partners. One extra one calls out "Face to face," then "Back to back," and finally "All change," whereupon they must get new partners, any extras doing same. Can be combined with fancy handshakes.

Another version has new partners get together, back to back. Then directions are given: "You have just seen a mouse, Face to face!" (The person must act out as directed.) Next directions may be: "You have just won a boxing match," and so on.

GAMELIKE MIXERS

Basketball Mixer. Using bean bag or soft rubber ball, two teams of five or more players are lined up, facing each other. (For large groups, divide them into several sets like this.) The captain of team A tosses ball or bean bag to team B. Whoever catches it holds it up. First player of team B must name person holding bean bag. For success: 2 points. For failure: 2 points to opposite team. Next, captain of team B tosses bag to team A, and first player of team A must identify.

Co-operative Spelling. Each person gets large card with letter of alphabet on it, also pin to put it on with. He also has card and pencil. He is to get together with other owners of letters to spell words. Writes those words on his card, rushes to spell other words. One with most words wins.

Hummer. Start out in pairs. On "GO" signal, each looks other in eye and starts humming. Continue until one has to take breath, which eliminates him. He must sit down. Other person finds another for elimination contest, and so on until one person is winner. (You can make other laugh, but cannot tickle him.) If there are those who spontaneously want to take the winner on at end, and you have time, let them do so.

Missing Persons Description. You have minute to get thoroughly acquainted with person who is your temporary partner. Everybody then separates. Leader calls on someone to describe person and see if all can guess who person was. Description should include: hair, eyes, size of nose, missing teeth, jewelry, color of shoes, etc.

Draw Your Neighbor. Everyone is furnished with pencil and paper or crayon, to draw picture of his neighbor. Pictures are posted, and group try to recognize them.

MIXERS INVOLVING NAMES

The Borrow Game. Players are seated in circle. (In very large group there can be several circles.) Every other player is odd. When piano plays chords, each person moves counterclockwise around circle as many positions as there were chords, and must introduce himself and borrow from that person some item.

Continue until players have accumulated three or four objects, when "REVERSE" is called out. Each must quickly return borrowed objects, thank donor, and sit down. Last one down pays forfeit.

Clock Mixer. To each person is given pencil and mimeographed large clock face, marked off into 12 pie-shaped segments. First fill in 12 divisions by having 12 persons autograph the section. When finished, leader will call out: "Go to 5 o'clock and talk about hobbies (or favorite foods, or yourselves) for 30 seconds."

Second version of this involves handing mimeographed sheet to players, with instructions: 1:00—A stranger to you. 2:00—Same color hair as yours. Then procedure is as described above.

Group Interviews. Superior get acquainted game. Around small circle (not more than 15, less if possible) have people introduce themselves, one at time, telling where they are from. Then *any person* in group may ask one just self-introduced *any questions* he chooses. (Person may decline to answer if he or she prefers.) Spend one or two minutes on each person and it will be surprising to see how much you can learn about that individual.

What's My Name? For steady group, small camp, or conference. At end of two or three days, announce that during day "What's my name?" will be played. Any person may walk up to another and say, "What's my name?" If he cannot give it, he must pay a forfeit.

It's a Nice Day. Sitting in circle (or circles) of not more than 15, first person says, to second person, "I, Bert Kessel, say it's a nice day." Second says to third, "Bert Kessel told me, Betty Watts, that it's a nice day." Third says to fourth: "Bert Kessel told Betty

Watts who told me, Bob Peterson, that it's a nice day,'' and so on until all have been successful. (More than 15 makes this a slow, abominable game.)

My Name Is . . . Like game above. "His name is Bill Beatty, her name is Catherine Allen, my name is Warren Willis,'' and so on around the circle. (If you get stuck, others may help you.)

Who Is This? On back of each person is pinned sheet of paper. You must first talk with person, get acquainted, then write remarks on his back. Later, these remarks are read aloud to see if person can be identified.

Introductions. Each person is to agree to introduce at least two members of group to each other, at least one of whom they do not know.

Collecting Autographs. Each person has sheet of paper and pencil. They are to get names and an additional description of 10 people (such as square, round, or oval face).

NO-PARTNER MIXERS

Longest Train. Get one or more persons out on floor and, when signal "Go" is given, see which one can form longest train by getting most people into his line, each with hands placed on shoulders of person ahead of him. Then do any of activities done in lines, like "I've Been Workin' on the Railroad,'' or Schottische Conga Line, without partners.

Shhhhh! Have everyone present say "Shhhhhhhh,'' getting all quiet. Then the leader takes someone's hand and says, "Come along''; that person does same to another person, and so on until all are in.

Musical Arches (Hawaiian London Bridge). One couple make 2-handed arch over heads of circle of players who move under arch as long as music plays. When music stops, they catch whoever is under arch and that person stands behind one of arch makers. Music resumes, and when stopped again person who was caught forms arch with one caught earlier. Next time two players are caught in two arches, and so on until all people are in couples from this arch procedure.

Bunny Hop (Rabbit Conga). This one has its own music, but could be done to many polka tunes. A line forms behind head person, each person with hands at waist of one ahead.
ACTION: Each person in line hops with left foot, and at same time flings right foot out to side; then hops again and draws foot back (but not touching floor); repeat, making twice that foot has been extended out and drawn back. With left foot, do same action, same number of times. Now with both feet together hop forward one hop, backward one hop, then three quick hops forward, twice as fast.

Conga Polka, Schottische. Basic polka or schottische step can be used by groups in conga line.

Ten Pretty Girls (Conga Line). World of Fun Record. In regular conga line, each person, with hands on shoulders of person ahead of him, or at waist of person ahead, raises left foot and puts his left toe ahead of normal position, then out to side of normal position, then steps behind right foot with left foot and puts weight on left foot, places right foot to right of normal position, and draws left foot to right one. Now he repeats same action, starting with right foot.

Next he takes four slow walking steps, followed by leaning backward with left foot extended forward (two counts), then backward (two counts), and a stamp-stamp-stamp (left foot, right foot, left foot) in place. Next time he starts with right foot, beginning from beginning.

A Circle Mixer. To march or polka music, group circles left in large circle. Stop music, get into groups by month of birthday, color of eyes, shoes, spectacle-wearers, or any others you devise. Play music between changes. Allow people to talk a little as they get into their groups. (In some cases, specify size of groups, for example, ''Not more than five of those who wear glasses'', or ''those who do not.'')

Get Acquainted Shout. Form circle without partners. Each person gets acquainted with person on each side of him. Ask all to shout out at same time name of person on their left; then on their right; then own name. Music starts, and group circles to left. While it is going, they are supposed to spot someone on opposite side of circle with whom they want to change places. When music stops, all rush for other spot across circle (a real mixer!) and process is repeated there, shouting names, then marching to music.

Introduction Circle. Leader introduces himself to person in circle who responds with his or her name, then continues to every fifth person around circle, introducing self. Each person who receives introduction then starts around circle *in opposite direction*, introducing himself or herself. Continue until number of introductions have been made, when leader calls out, ''Everybody home.'' Last one back to place becomes leader next time, and introduction process is begun again.

I've Been Workin' on the Railroad. This musical game requires no partners, and can be done in several styles. For family nights and children's groups, use it in choo-choo line, one person at head as engine, and rest with hands on shoulders or at waist of person ahead, as cars.

Sometimes it is done around circle, people with arms linked, two couples, side by side. May be done in trio form also, with center person moving forward after each horn blowing, to make it progressive.

ACTION: All sing ''I've been workin' on the railroad'' as they march along. Then they stop and place left heel out to left, bring it back to place, then right heel out, bring it back, and do two knee bends, as they sing line: ''All the live-long day. Hey!'' Continue with this pattern, marching on one line, doing the footwork on the second line, always with the ''Hey!'' on second knee bend. Exception: At end, instead of knee bends, do two toots on Dinah's horn, (''Dinah, blow your horn. Toot! Toot!'') pulling an imaginary cord to toot horn. *Repeat as often as desired.*

Snake Dance. As lively march gets people in mood, ask them to clap, stand, then join in snake dance. Leader takes hand, then that person takes another, and soon everybody is in circle.

Come Along. This game is usually played in circle, standing. Leader holds out hand to someone and says, "Come along." That person takes another hand with "Come along." On signal, "Go home," all return to places, and It tries to get place.

To do this cumulatively, without people standing, explain briefly how it is played, and then proceed as in Snake Dance, above, until all are in who want to be in.

WAYS OF GETTING PARTNERS

Piecing Together Objects Torn or Cut Apart. Hearts, for Valentine's Day; hatchets, for Washington's Birthday; pumpkins, cats or witches, for Hallowe'en; leaves from old magazines; words of songs, proverbs, or jokes written on paper or cardboard. These are cut apart irregularly, half being given to men, half to girls. Partners are matched up.

Sing a Song. You will find another singing same song as you, or humming same tune.

Famous Combinations. (Cut them in half.)
Persons: Antony and Cleopatra; Columbus and Queen Isabella.
Foods: Peaches and cream; salt and pepper; corned beef and cabbage; ham and eggs; bread and butter; liver and bacon.

Same Trade. Each person has a list of several occupations on slip of paper. Each goes around trying to find partner who is acting out an occupation of bus driver, ditch digger, truck driver, log chopper, violinist, house painter, and so on. Several players will have same list of occupations on their slip as you do and will have chosen one of them. Find the person who has made same choice as you have made.

Blindfold Line. Half stand in line. The other half are blindfolded, walk down the line shaking hands until they decide on partner. They must decide as they go down—no turning back. Continue until all have partners.

COUPLE MIXERS

Don't just say "Get a partner" (unless the group is small, and know each other very, very well). Use some of these methods to get into groups:

Accumulation. While all are standing in circle, one person marches around inside circle as music plays. When music stops, this person gets partner from circle and marches, as music begins again. At next music stop, each of two get partners, making four people on inside. Continue marching with them; when music stops, each gets new partner, to make eight people in action. Continue until all are in circle.

Circulation Group Starter. Tell group that you want them to get some circulation in their feet. Ask them to rise, reach as high as possible, reach out in front as far as possible, reach out to each side. (Now turn up sound of very peppy march or polka record, or have it played on piano.) Ask them to start walking, around circle to left, then to right, then all girls or women to center and back; all men or boys to center, find a girl, swing her, and all promenade. (In some cases two girls will need to be partners.) Now you have them in couples.

Clap Starter. In difficult situation such as gym, play good, rhythmic record and have people stand and clap. Continuing clapping, get men or boys to come to floor, then girls and women, who make ring around men and boys. Have two circles move in opposite directions until music stops. They are now facing their first partner. With simple routine line this may be done: "Forward and bow," "Right hand turn," "Left hand turn," "Both hands turn," "Swing," "Move on to the next girl," in manner of Virginia Reel.

Musical Handshake. Two circles of equal numbers of people move in opposite directions (one inside other). When they stop, each person introduces himself to other, tells a little about self.

Crazy Handshakes. Procedure as in Musical Handshake. After introducing each other, leader shows group how to do fancy handshakes:

1. MODEL T FORD. Shake hands by cranking laboriously.
2. PUMP-HANDLE STYLE. Each pumps other's hand vigorously.
3. FISHERMAN'S. Each makes hand very limp, wiggles them back and forth.
4. AUTOMATIC. Each takes hands very limply. "No clutch."
5. PAUL BUNYAN. Clasp hands in regular fashion, take own thumb in left hand, and saw back and forth (still holding hands). When the tree is sawed down, yell "Timberrr!"
6. BOXER'S. Shake own hands, above head, in various directions, as if to crowd.
7. CHINESE. Shake own hand, bow three times.
8. BASEBALL. This is like choosing up, using bat. One person starts by making fist, thumb up. Next person takes that thumb in his fist, thumbs up. Continue until hands are stacked four high, then shake them up and down.
9. SHAKE LEFT HANDS ONLY.
10. SHAKE HANDS, SIDE TO SIDE, ONLY.
11. MILKMAID STYLE. Men or boys interlace own fingers, turn hands upside down, thumbs pointed down. Girls are to take hold, milkmaid style.
12. HAND SLAP. One person extends hands out, palms toward floor. Other extends hands, fingers together, palms up. Object: For one whose hands are below to slap back of hands of one whose hands are above, before that person can withdraw hands. When he is successful, they shift roles. Play two or three times only in this formation.

O'Grady Starter. Play "O'Grady says" in usual fashion. That is, leader gives command to group, who follow command if O'Grady said to do it, but remain motionless unless command is preceded by magic words, "O'Grady says . . ." Finally O'Grady says, "All boys to the middle of the room." Then "All girls make a circle around them, and all boys face the girls." Then they are in position for any circle partner game.

Go Between. Ask each man to go between two girls. Girl on his right is his partner, other goes to lost and found department in center. Then encourage others on sidelines to come and take a partner, or let lost and founds go out to take a partner for themselves. Or they may couple up, two girls together, where necessary.

Scatter Promenade. When group is in couples, call for them to circle four, any four. (This means any two couples getting together.) Then do one figure and call "Scatter Promenade," whereupon they must "promenade" to another couple anywhere and circle with them.

Partner Grab (when extras are present). While lively music plays, two circles (one inside other) move in opposite directions, boys or men in one circle, girls or women in other. When music stops, each person grabs nearest player as partner. Extras go to center of circle. When music starts again, they join proper circle.

My Name's Jane (mixer in trios). Get into groups of three, then promenade in three's around large circle. While marching to tune of "Goodnight, Ladies," outside ones in trios (farthest from center of circle) sing, "My name's _____." Next, inside circle (persons closest to center) respond, "My name's _____"; last, middle ones sing, "My name's _____." All sing "Let's go and meet the rest." Center person in each trio moves forward to join two players ahead. All skip or march forward singing "Merrily we roll along. . . ." Then the introduction process starts again. (Leader may ask outside circle to move forward instead of middle one, or inside one.)

Easy March. Ask all to rise, take one step forward, right face, start marching. When they are on floor, have them join hands, circle left, circle right, march single file again. Then men step one step to inside of circle and march in opposite direction from ladies. When call comes to "Swing" they swing with next lady they meet, and march together counterclockwise.

Nursery Rhymes. There are two circles, men's inside of women's (or boys' inside of girls'). Idea is to take nursery rhyme and say or sing it, one line to each person you meet, everyone acting out words where appropriate, such as "Jack Spratt" or "Little Miss Muffett."

Creative Mixer. Divide into small groups and give group several minutes to take song and work out action to it, mixer style.

Name March. All are sitting in circle, no vacant chairs. Person in center has names of all. Scrambles names, then pick names at random and reads them aloud. These people stand and march around, counterclockwise, inside circle of chairs as march music is played. When music stops suddenly everybody, including center person, rushes for chair. One left out becomes "It" in center.

"Big Wheel" Grand March. All people arriving are given, instead of their own names (or in addition), name of famous person in history, fiction, the Bible, politics, movies, radio, or television. They are in two circles, one inside other. When music plays, circles go in opposite directions. When it stops, the two are to carry on an appropriate conversation for characters they are portraying.

Musical Arches. Players form single circle. Two persons make London Bridge arch. All march under arch as music plays. When it stops, whoever is caught goes into center of circle. Next time, person under arch joins with first-caught person, and the two form another arch. Continue catching people in each arch until all are in a double circle.

Circle Four. To good, lively march music all players start marching in circle. When leader calls out, "Circle four," they must quickly get into fours and circle in fours until another number is called. If this is "Circle six" some must scatter to other circles. "Circle all" gets all in circle again. (Folks left out at any call go to center until another call is given.)

Hello Grand Right and Left. As music plays for circle of couples who know how to do grand right and left, they move about, greeting each person they meet with "hello," until they get to their partners on opposite side. There they bow to partner, continue beyond partner with more "hellos" until they meet again, then they promenade some more. Same pattern may be used for "Good-bye" or "Good night."

Missionary Barrel. Each person is to come wearing some clothes he will not need beyond tonight. As music plays, there are two circles, one inside other. Everybody marches around, and circles continue until all have seen clothes. When music stops, two persons facing each other must exchange as many clothes as they dare, and wear them for rest of evening.

Name Tag March. In meetings using name tags, each person takes off his tag, drops it on floor, toward center of circle. Then single circle moves to music about halfway around until the music stops. Each person is to pick up a name tag and try to find its owner, get acquainted. Name may be shouted out.

Ten Little Handshakes.
THE SONG: (Tune is "Ten Little Indians")

> One little, two little, three little handshakes;
> Four little, five little, six little handshakes;
> Seven little, eight little, nine little handshakes;
> Ten little handshakes all.

FORMATION: Two circles, one inside other. They move slowly in opposite directions as people sing and walk along, shaking hands. On tenth handshake, give specially hearty one and get acquainted.

FORMATION MIXERS USING MUSIC

Do-Si-Do Mixer. Using lively march, polka, or square dance music (all in circle):

1. All join hands and balance in (walk to center four steps and back). *Repeat.*
2. Do-si-do with corner, do-si-do with partner (back to back).
3. Allemande left with corner, allemande right with partner.
4. Swing the corner and promenade with corner.

Hello and Good-Bye (to march or Glow Worm, or Four Leaf Clover)
FORMATION: Double circle, men on inside. Circles faces counterclockwise; man holds girl's left hand in his right hand.
ACTION: (1) Walk forward four steps. (2) Partners face each other, each walks backward four steps. (3) Each man now moves toward girl who was at his left, and she toward

him. (4) These new partners join right hands and walk around each other with one complete turn. Now they are in promenade position, ready to move forward again.

NOTES: It is helpful to call out one-word or two-word description of action, as: (1) "Forward." (2) "Part" or "Apart." (3) "New Girl." (4) "Turn."

Irish Washerwoman Mixer

FORMATION: Single circle, facing in.
THE CALL:

1. "All join hands and into the middle,
2. With your big foot keep time to the fiddle,
3. When you get back, remember my call,
4. Swing on the corner and promenade all."

ACTION: 1. All walk to center four steps. 2. All stamp foot four counts. 3. All back to place four steps. 4. Swing corner once and promenade (16 counts in all for promenade).

Texas Schottische

FORMATION: Double circle, facing counterclockwise. Man reaches across girl's shoulder to take her left hand in his, across his chest to take her right hand in his.

ACTION: Each person takes step diagonally forward, slightly toward center with left foot; draws right foot up to left foot; steps again with left foot, pauses one count, to one measure of music. Now each does same with right foot leading, draws left foot to it, steps with right again, pauses.

Now all do four slow walking steps, left, right, left, right. Last, each person puts down left heel (count 1) then toe (count 2), and girl takes three quick walking steps, dropping right hand, going over to left side of man (pausing on count 4). Same action with right heel and toe and three more fast walking steps. She completes her turn, ending up at right of man who was behind her, with hands raised, ready for him to take her and begin again, with her left hand in his.

You say: "Left, slide, left and right, slide, right, and walk, walk, walk, walk. Heel and toe and walk, walk, walk. Heel and toe and walk, walk, walk."

VARIATIONS:

1. Instead of four slow walking steps, do eight fast running ones.
2. Do everything double time. (Instead of "heel and toe and," do "heel-toe, heel-toe," and so on.)
3. Instead of passing girl back, keep her one time, send her back next.
4. Do opening steps like Ten Pretty Girls, up to "heel and toe and halfway round."
5. Partner-stealing version. As girl turns and faces halfway round, extra girls (who are on outside of circle) beat them to their partners. Those left out wait until next time. For men to steal, they stand in men's circle and receive girl as she comes back.

Jessie Polka (Any tempo polka record will do.)

FORMATION: Various. In couples, skating position; or without partners in conga line, or side by side, 3, 4 or more abreast. Step is same.

ACTION: With weight on right foot, point left heel forward, put it back in place. Shift weight to left foot and point right heel forward, bring it back to place, right toe backward, then bring it to place; shift weight to right foot and extend left foot forward, then bring it back diagonally in front of right foot with a fast sweeping motion; then lead with left foot for four polka steps. (Step with left, bring right foot to it, step with left again, pause; repeat same footwork, beginning with right foot.) Continue as long as desired.

Patty Cake Polka ("Little Brown Jug")

FORMATION: Double circle, men facing partners with their backs to center of circle, both with arms outstretched, hands joined.

ACTION: Starting with man's left, girl's right: touch heel to floor, then toe, then heel, then toe and do four slides around circle, counterclockwise. Repeat with opposite foot, coming back to place with same action.

PATTY CAKE: Partners face and clap right hands three times, left hands with each other three times, both hands three times, then slap knees three times. Hook right arms, walk around (or polka) and the man moves to next girl to his left (counterclockwise) to begin again.

Clap Marlene (adapted and simplified from Lili Marlene, "Susan's Gavotte")

FORMATION: Double circle of partners, men on inside, facing counterclockwise, inside hands joined.

ACTION:

1. Beginning with outside foot, take four walking steps forward, then partners face quickly and continue to slide four quick slides in same direction. Same action, back to place.
2. Clap own hands, then right on partner's right. Own hands, then left on partner's left; own, then both hands on partner's hands; clap own once again.
3. Link right arms and circle halfway around each other; left arms and back to place.
4. Repeat No. 2 exactly.
5. Link right arms, go all way around partner, man moves to next girl to his left, to begin from beginning.

Captain Jinks Mixer (World of Fun Record)

FORMATION: Single circle of partners, facing center.
ACTION:

1. Walk eight steps clockwise.
2. Walk eight steps, counterclockwise.
3. Four steps toward center and back, hands joined.
4. Swing corner person, who becomes new partner.

Jingle Bells Mixer

FORMATION: Pairs or couples in double circle, facing counterclockwise, inside hands joined.

ACTION: Eight walking steps forward, then eight steps backward. Four slides counterclockwise, then four back to place; then right shoulder do-si-do (back to back).

ON "JINGLE BELLS": On partner's hands, clap right hand three times, left three times, both five times, then link right arms, and go once completely around each other. *Repeat* Jingle Bells action, this time ending with man facing another girl, one to his left.

Circle Virginia Reel

FORMATION: Double circle, men with backs to center, facing partners, six feet separating them.

ACTION: (Calls are in quotation marks.)

1. "Forward and bow." Partners take three steps toward each other and bow or curtsey, back to place.
2. "Right hand swing." Raise right hand, join with partner, circle around each other, return to place.
3. "Left hand swing," "Both hands swing," Right arm swing," Left arm swing," all based on No. 2 with appropriate hands or arms used.
4. "Right halfway, left back." Swing around, right arms, halfway around; shift to left arm and return to place.
5. "Right shoulder, do-si-do." Partners advance toward each other, pass right shoulders, go around each other back to back, return to place.
6. "Left shoulder, do-si-do." Same, with left shoulder passing.
7. "Bow to the next girl." EAch man advances to girl at left and bows to her. Then begin with No. 2, above, and continue through No. 7, repeating as long as desired or until music ends.

Freeze. Novelty action. When music is stopped suddenly, each couple must freeze where they are and remain motionless. Those who move are eliminated. See who can last longest.

Tray Mixer

FORMATION: Two lines, men-and-women, down length of room and close to one side of it. Two lines face three chairs. Leader sits in center chair, and first two persons in line of opposite sex to leader come and sit in chairs. He gives tray to one and polkas, schottisches, waltzes (whatever the music is) off with other one. That person holding tray goes to center chair, and two others come to sit in other chairs, with same procedure as at first. To stop game, stop tray passing.

Good Night, Ladies

FORMATION: Double circle of partners, men on inside, women on outside, facing each other.

ACTION: As all sing, men bow low to their partners (who curtsey) as they sing first "Good night, ladies." Then men move to left to next lady for second "Good night, ladies," move third time for third "Good night, ladies," and fourth time "We're going to leave you now." Take this one for partner and skip or march around circle, promenade fashion. *Now repeat all action with verses* "Farewell, ladies," and "Sweet dreams, ladies." Emotion at parting is sometimes exaggerated for effect.

Following this action, many groups close with fellowship circle (all standing side by side, hands crossed in front, holding hands with those on either side) and sing quiet hymns, spirituals, and perhaps a prayer.

Standing Good Night Ladies. Group stand in circle, hands crossed in front and joined with neighbors on both sides. All bow low to left on first "Good night, ladies," to right on second one, toward middle on third. On "Merrily . . ." all wave joined hands up and down, gently.

Good Night Grand Right and Left

FORMATION: Single circle of partners, ready to say good night.

ACTION: As they go through Grand Right and Left figure, each person says, "Good night" to each person he or she meets, until meeting partner. Bow to partner, continue beyond with more good nights. Second time, swing partner and promenade as directed.

Mixers for Twos and Threes in Same Circle. To accommodate extras, adapt some of your favorite couple mixers into trios, and mix couples and trios in the same circle, suggests Jay Spurlin, Tatum, New Mexico.

Texas Schottische for twos and threes is a good illustration. At the beginning the twos and threes are intermixed around circle, facing counterclockwise. Proceed according to directions. At partner change, man sends back his "one" or "two" partners, whichever the case may be. This way, no one is left out.

Others may be adapted to trios. Take "The Thief." Stand in trios, instead of couples, around circle, facing center. Thief steals two partners instead of one. Or have thieves work in pairs, stealing one person to be their middle man.

For "Oh! Susanna" have players in trios, facing center. Girls go to center, four steps and back; boys or men the same. Repeat. Then promenade, counterclockwise, in trios. On last four beats, center person moves ahead to next trio, and all "circle up" once more. (This drops the Grand Right and Left, making action simpler.) Try this idea with other mixers.

Quiet Games

7

For the user's convenience, the more than 300 games and ideas in this long chapter have been grouped in certain categories which give a clue to the situations to which they are best adapted. The sixteen kinds are listed as follows:

Games for Preschool Children
Quiet Games for Circles or Small
  Groups
One-Less-Seat Games
Games, Standing or Walking
Cumulative Games
Passing Games
Mystery, Puzzler, and Accomplice
  Games

Games with Proverbs
Creative, Improvising Games
Fun with Art Materials
Magazine Games
Blindfold Games
Balloon Games
Forfeits or Consequences
Novel or Quiet Relays and Races
Physical Feats and Stunts

GAMES FOR YOUNG CHILDREN

There are activities for young children in other sections, such as equipment games, crafts. Here are some miscellaneous ideas.

Tepee, Tent. Use tripod, card table, tree branch, and throw sheet or blanket over it for children to play Indian.

Bubbles. Children love to blow bubbles from soapy water (with a few drops of glycerin added for strength). You can also buy bottles of commercially prepared bubble liquid.

Two Little Bluebirds. Paste little pieces of paper on forefingers, place them on table. "Two little bluebirds sitting on a fence. One named Jack and one named Jill!" (Indicate which is which.) "Fly away, Jack." (Throw it over your shoulder, replace with middle finger on table.) "Fly away, Jill." (Same idea.)

Pinning the Tail on the Donkey. This old party favorite of having children blindfolded and trying to pin tail on donkey can be adapted seasonally to: pin cherry on tree, pin mouth on Jack-o'-lantern, pin beard on Santa.

"Did You Ever See a Farmer?" Sing, having farmer do his chores of digging, sowing, driving tractor.

Imitating Animals. Little children like to make noises of animals, later to act out animals in action.

Marching. To music, even two small children can amuse themselves marching, especially if adult will help them get mental image of themselves doing some grand thing.

Water Play. Little children like to play in water, to pour, splash it on each other, whether outdoors or in bathtub. Little boats can be made of English walnut halves with toothpick as mast, triangular piece of paper as sail.

Hunting. Hide objects, let children hunt for them. Give hints if necessary.

GAMES FOR CIRCLES OR SMALL GROUPS

These games, many of which can be played around a table, are mostly the kind which challenges the player to be quick on the trigger—with a maximum of mental alertness and a minimum of physical energy to be expended.

Cackleberry

Seated in small circle (not over 10 players) each one takes a motion which can be done easily, repeated in rhythm four times. All check with each other to see that there is no duplication. Sample motions: pat head, clap hands, flip ear, pull nose.

Then they practice chant: CACKLEBERRY, CACKLEBERRY, CACKLEBERRY, NOW! (There are several versions, like Checkerberry.) Now they put this chant together with their motions, for practice.

The object is to look at person at your left, make your motion four times, then shift to motion your left hand neighbor is doing, every fourth time. In other words, after the word NOW in the chant, you change to the motion your left-hand neighbor has just been doing. If this is done accurately, each person gets back his own motion in as many changes as there are people in the circle. Good table game.

(Age, 9 up . . . Group, 5-10 . . . Time, 10 min.)

Rainbow Game

Colors of rainbow are, of course, red, orange, yellow, green, blue, indigo, violet. Starting around circle, first person names something red, next one something orange, next yellow, and so on. If you miss, stand behind your chair. See who can stay in longest.

(Age, 6 up . . . Group, 5-30 . . . Time, 10-15 min.)

Stick Rhythm

Any number of players are seated in circle on floor, six to twelve preferable. Four round smooth sticks or dowels, about 14 inches long and $\frac{3}{4}$ inch thick are passed to right around circle in slow waltz rhythm of piano or recorded music.

Two persons beside each other hold stick in each hand. Counting one, two, three to music, bring sticks down to floor on "one," toss stick in right hand to person on right on "two," and toss stick in left hand on "three." Sticks are caught in corresponding hands of next person; for example, first stick is tossed and caught in right hand and second stick is tossed and caught in left hand.

(Age, 9 up . . . Size of group, 5-10 . . . Time, 15-30 min.)

Air, Land, Water, Fire. "It" tosses into lap of player knotted handkerchief or other object and calls "Air," "Land," "Water," or "Fire," counts to 10 quickly. Receiving player must name a dweller of the element named (remaining silent for "fire") before count of 10 or become It.

(Age, 9 up . . . Group, 5-30 . . . Time, 10 min.)

Snip. Similar game. It spells a three-letter word, like "Dog" or "Cat" and pronounces it, then counts to 12. The person whom he indicates in the circle must give a word beginning with each of those letters or be It.

(Age, 9 up . . . Group, 8-20 . . . Time, 10 min.)

Bird, Beast, Fish. Similar, also. On challenge, player must name a bird, beast or fish before count of 10 or become It.

(Age, 9 up . . . Group, 8-30 . . . Time, 10 min.)

Shopping. "I'm going to Columbus. What can I buy?" says It, quickly counting to 10, having indicated player in circle who is to answer. That person must answer with something beginning with "C," first letter of city.

(Age, 9 up . . . Group, 8-30 . . . Time, 10 min.)

Dutch Band. Each player in circle is assigned instrument to play in pantomime, such as fiddle, trombone, trumpet. Several may be playing same instrument. Leader signals play by putting his thumbs in ears and waggling fingers, whereupon all play their instruments. If he shifts to any instrument, however, those players must waggle fingers as he did. If he catches someone making mistake, he changes places, and that person becomes new band leader.

(Age, 9 up . . . Group, any size . . . Time, 5-10 min.)

Fun with Numbers:

Take any number, for example, 50

Double it	100
Add any even number	42
	142
Take half	71
	71
Subtract original	50
	21

You simply double answer and you will arrive at the number that was added (42).

(Age, 9 up . . . Group, any size . . . Time, 10 min.)

This Is My Nose. Seated in circle with It in center, player points to his eye and says, "This is my nose." Before he counts 10, person who is approached must put his finger on his nose and say, "This is my eye," or else become It.

(Age, 6 up . . . Group, 5-30 . . . Time, 10 min.)

We Don't Like Peas. Each person is to try to find something that you do like, as you question them around circle. You like pears, apples, turnips, because all contain letter "P." Gradually players will get it. (Other letters, such as "B's," "T's" may be used.)
(Age, 9 up . . . Group, 5-30 . . . Time, 10-15 min.)

Fox, Gun, Hunter. Gun (represented by aiming) kills fox. Fox (wiggle thumbs in ears) can outrun hunter, and Hunter (represented by folded arms) can shoot gun. Thus each is superior to one other. Leader calls signal, "One, Two, Three, GO!" and action begins. Here are three uses of game.

1. Two players face each other. This could be in dozens or hundreds of "twos" around auditorium, in meeting, or at table. On signal, "Go!" each immediately represents one of three. See who gets point for that time.
2. Two teams play. Each team gets into huddle and decides which of three entire group will represent. Two teams then line up. Leader gives starting signal, "One, two, three, GO!" and on "Go" entire team represents its chosen symbol to opposite. Play for 5-7-9 times. Ties do not count as a time.
3. Leader walks around circle of not over 25 players, makes one of signs quickly to one person, who before count of ten must return superior one, or become It.
   In all cases it is good to have group practice symbols several times. Sometimes it is good for leader to represent one (such as gun) and have group quickly do superior one back to him.
   (Age, 6 up . . . Group, 5-30 . . . Time, 10-15 min.)

Laughing Hyenas. In two teams, one group is tops, one bottoms, as plate is spun in full view of them. When spun plate lands, bottom up, bottoms laugh heartily, others are silent. If top side is up, tops laugh. Any player laughing out of turn joins other team.
(Age, preschool up . . . Group, 5-50 . . . Time, 5-10 min.)

Roman Numeral Flash Cards. Make large numeral cards with Roman numerals on them. Hold them up one at a time. Person who calls correct number first gets card. See who gets most cards. May be played in sides; side getting most cards, wins.
(Age, 9 up . . . Group, any size . . . Time, 10 min.)

Letter Cards (Flash Cards). Have complete set of large cards (quick way is to make them with liquid black shoe polish) and use them in any one of following ways:

1. Tell story, hold up letter, and ask for name of city, car, famous person, beginning with that letter. Weave into story. Whoever speaks first holds letter. Person or side getting most, wins.
2. "See who can name something you would find in grocery store beginning with this letter." (Then hold it up.)
3. Similar idea, seeing who can name Bible persons, places, events beginning with letters you display, one at a time.
4. Or call for names of any of the following beginning with letter held up by leader:

Vegetables

Names of athletes

Scientists

Book titles

Characters from Shakespeare

Actors

Authors

Presidents, Kings or Queens

Lakes or seas

Rivers

Minerals

Flowers

Fish

Trees

Birds

Animals

What you find in a garage

Musical terms

Nature objects

(Age, 6 up . . . Group, any size . . . Time, 10 min.)

Room Scavenger Hunt. Divide into teams. Each has list of several items (up to ten) hidden around room, or in building or close by. Each list is different, and no team may take any object except those on its own list. See who gets most complete list.
(Age, 9 up . . . Group, 3-10 . . . Time, 10-20 min.)

Camouflage. Divide into couples. Each is to take trip through room or building to discover ten items listed which are in plain sight but camouflaged by naturalness of place where located, such as red comb on red divan, brown penny on brown window sill, gold ring on lampshade ball. When person or couple discovers object, they make only mental note for time being, lest they give its location away to others. (Excellent game for getting people acquainted with rooms, buildings, facilities, in schools, camps, churches, or community centers.)
(Age, 9 up . . . Group, 2 each . . . Time, 15-20 min.)

Elephant (and variations). Group of not over 30, seated in circle. It in center suddenly points to any person, who must make trunk with both fists. Persons on each side of him must make elephant ears by cupping hands and placing at his ears. Last one to do his job becomes It. Many groups improvise their variations like these:

RABBIT. Middle one eats carrot, side people form ears.

DONKEY. Same, except that middle one brays, nods head.

EARLY BIRD. Center one puts finger in mouth, side people form wings.

DUCK. Center person makes bill with both hands, others peck at him with fingers.

SPIRIT OF '76. Center one pantomimes holding flag; one at his left beats drum, one at his right plays fife.

FIRECRACKER (involving five players). Ones on each side say BOOOM. Ones on each side of Booms hold hands over BOOM's ears to keep out noise.

BANDIT. Center one raises both hands, and persons on each side raise the hand closest to center one.

Rhythm. Numbered players are seated in circle, with marked "Head" and "Foot," No. 1 at head to start. Principle is to keep in rhythm. All at same time SLAP legs with both hands, CLAP hands, and first player calls his own number (at same time SNAPPING fingers on left hand) then calls number of another player, such as 6, at same time with SNAP of fingers of right hand. Rhythm is continued, with No. 6 calling own number on left-hand snap, another number for right-hand snap. Continue until one player breaks rhythm. He or she goes to foot, all others seated below that player move one position toward head. Each player takes number of chair, rather than keeping same number all the time.

(Age, 9 up . . . Group, 10-30 . . . Time, 10-15 min.)

California Game. Another version of Rhythm calls for two slaps on legs, two claps, one snap of right fingers as a word is given, pause, and then a number is called as left fingers snap. (On snap of right fingers, word is given, such as "egg," and after pause, number of a player is called, such as 12.) Rhythm is continued, and on snap of right fingers No. 12 must give word beginning with last letter of previous word, "egg," which might be "gum," then calls another number on snap of left fingers. Words may not be repeated. Other counting is as in Rhythm.

(Age, 9 up . . . Group, 5-30 . . . Time, 10-15 min.)

Indian Rhythm. Around small circle, such as table, each person chooses two-word Indian name. All introduce themselves around circle at least twice, so that names become familiar. At start, rhythm is begun by four slow, steady beats on table or on own legs, whereupon starting player gives own name, like "Red Cloud" and name of another person, "Running Deer." Then after four more beats, Running Deer gives own name and another. In this there is no penalty for missing. It is fun to see if you can maintain rhythm. Faster way to play is to eliminate interval of four beats, tossing names back and forth fast.

(Age, 6 up . . . Group, 8-20 . . . Time, 10 min.)

Football Game. A large circle is chalked on floor and players sit with their feet right up to circle. There are two teams, divided by line across center of circle. The object is to kick football (or other ball) from middle of the circle across center line, and into the opponent's territory. Such a successful kick calls for one point. Game is 10-15 points. Make your own rules as needed.

(Age, 9 up . . . Group, 10-30 . . . Time, 10-15 min.)

Simon Says. Players sit in circle, or if played in schoolroom, sit at their respective desks. Each player makes a fist of each hand with thumb extended. One is chosen for leader, whom others follow.

Leader says, "Simon says, 'Thumbs up!'" whereupon he places his own fists before him with thumbs upward. Players must all do likewise. Leader then says, "Simon says, 'Thumbs down!'" whereupon he turns his own hands over so that tips of thumbs point down, others imitating him.

He may then say, "Simon says, 'Thumbs wiggle-waggle!'" whereupon he places his fists before him with thumbs upward and moves thumbs sideways, players imitating him.

If at any time leader omits words "Simon says," and goes through movements simply with words, "Thumbs up," "Thumbs down," or "Wiggle-waggle," players must keep their hands still and not imitate his movements. Any player imitating him under these circumstances must either pay forfeit or become leader, or both, as may be decided on beforehand.

(Age, 6 up . . . Group, any size . . . Time, 5-10 min.)

Gossip. Seated in small circle, one player whispers to neighbor that "Jim was seen coming in a few nights ago under suspicious circumstances at 3:00 A.M." Neighbor then relays the gossip around circle. Fun comes in comparing original statement with what got around circle. (This may be made seasonal: "There's a story abroad that George Washington really didn't cut down a cherry tree.")

(Age, 9 up . . . Group, 10-30 . . . Time, 5-10 min.)

Spin the Bottle. As players sit in circle, they spin bottle in middle of circle, first asking it question which can be answered by pointing. Bottle points to proper one to answer question, like "Who is the prettiest?" Bottle can also point to folks to do stunts, tasks.

(Age, preschool, up . . . Size of Group, 5-20 . . . Time, 5-10 min.)

Human Tic-Tac-Toe. In large circle of 20 or more players place nine chairs in middle, three in row, three rows, as in Tic-tac-toe. There are two teams and each captain of each team, one at a time, sends one of his players out to sit in certain chair. Object is to get three of your team in a row, as in Tic-tac-toe.

Rhythmic Spelling. Best in circle of not more than 20 players. All may participate simultaneously, or may be single individuals.

In spelling word, player hops simultaneously with both feet off floor to represent consonant, and with one foot raised to represent vowel. Words with interesting rhythms have repeated letters, like Tennessee, Mississippi. It is fun for all, simultaneously, to hop and spell words such as those indicated.

Another version of this is to have people spell out their names, then tell something about themselves, as get-acquainted activity.

Another is to have them spell out word for others to guess. Similarly it could be guessing game with hidden object of seasonal significance, like clock (New Year's), heart (Valentine's), flag (Independence Day), gobbler (Thanksgiving).

(Age, 6 up . . . Size of Group, 5-30 . . . Time, 5-15 min.)

ONE-LESS-SEAT GAMES

In nearly all these games there is one less chair in the circle than there are players, and there is a leader or starter person whose object is to get a seat (or else to exchange places with someone in the circle).

Fruit Basket (basic game). Each person sitting in circle bears name of some fruit. When leader calls names of two fruits, they must change and he tries to get a seat. Signal for all to change is: "Fruit basket turnover," whereupon all change, and leader tries to get seat.

(Age, preschool up . . . Group, 5-15 . . . Time, 10 min.)

Numbers Change. See Fruit Basket. Same idea except that persons are numbered instead of named as fruits.

(Age, 9 up . . . Group, 5-15 . . . Time, 10 min.)

Blowout. Similar to Fruit Basket, except that players are named parts of an automobile, and they fall in line behind leader until he calls "blowout," when all try for seat, including leader. "Traffic cop" is signal for all to change. Similar titles are found in Stagecoach, Taxicab, Post Office.

(Age, preschool up . . . Group, 5-15 . . . Time, 10 min.)

Danish Fish Game. Similar to "Blowout" in that "It" couple walks around room, where couples are sitting with their chairs facing in random directions, and calls off names of fishes. (Couples secretly choose names of fishes for themselves.) When their name is called, they fall in line and march behind lead couple. Signal for return to seats is, "The ocean is stormy." Since there is one less pair of seats than players, last couple is It. (Signal for all to move: "The ocean is calm.")

(Age, preschool up . . . Group, 10-50 . . . Time, 10 min.)

Honeymoon Express. Based on similar idea, this game calls for chairs arranged like a train, with couples seated together, each couple having state as destination which they have chosen secretly. "It" couple start out (in role of conductor and trainman) calling off names of states, and couples get off train to join in march around train. Signal for "Everybody march" is "Niagara Falls," and that for reboarding is "All aboard." Last couple is It for next try.

(Age, 6 up . . . Group, 10-50 . . . Time, 10 min.)

Drop the Keys (mixer). Leader greets player seated in circle by exchanging names with him or her, and the two start in opposite directions around circle, speaking to every fourth or fifth player, who in turn does same thing. When several are on their feet, leader suddenly drops bunch of keys, and all rush for places. Last one is It next time, taking keys.

(Age, 6 up . . . Group, 10-50 . . . Time, 10 min.)

Follow Me. "It" greets person seated in circle with "Follow me." Player does. Continue until several are in line, then call "Go home," and last one home starts next time.

(Age, preschool up . . . Group, 10-100 . . . Time, 10 min.)

Come Along. Same as "Follow Me," except that person says, "Come along" and takes him by hand. Then that person says to another, "Come along," and so on.

(Age, preschool up . . . Group, 10-100 . . . Time, 10 min.)

Rose Garden. Players are numbered off by fours around circle, named "Red Roses," "White Roses," "Pink Roses," "Ramblers." "It" calls for two kinds to change places and he tries to get seat in process.

(Age, 6 up . . . Group, 5-30 . . . Time, 10 min.)

How Do You Like Your Neighbor? Players ask names of those seated on both sides of them in circle. (If they do not know each other well, number off.) "It" in center says to player, "How do you like your neighbors?" "Fine," he says, whereupon all change seats and It tries to get seat. If, however, he says, "I don't like 'em," then he is asked to designate whom he'd like to have for neighbors. His present neighbors and those he has named (or numbers called) must change places and It tries for seat. Last one is It.

(Age, 9 up . . . Group, 5-30 . . . Time, 10 min.)

Who Are Your Neighbors? (mixer). This version calls for person challenged to give names for his neighbors, or else become It. Then It proceeds as above.

(Age, 6 up . . . Group, 5-30 . . . Time, 10 min.)

Hot Potato (also called Hot Towel, Hot Rag, Hot Handkerchief). Object such as handkerchief is passed from one to another around circle, seated very close together. Whoever lets It get object becomes It, or whoever touched it last before It recovers. Object may be ball, piece of sponge, or any other object. It may be passed or thrown.
(Age, preschool up . . . Group, 8-30 . . . Time, 10 min.)

Swat. It, with rolled-up newspaper in hand, walks around circle of seated players, eventually strikes one with the swatter, rushes and places swatter on stool or bench in center of circle. As the struck player tries to get swatter and swat It, It tries to get the vacated seat before he can be swatted. If swatter rolls off bench, It must replace it, even though this puts him in danger of getting swatted. If It gets vacant chair without being swatted, the loser becomes It.

Bird Game. Each chair is named for bird. When kind of bird is called by leader for which your chair is labeled, you clap hands. Then when leader calls out, "Fly, bird, fly," you fly to chair vacated by another bird, taking on that new bird name. Leader may try to get place (in which case one left out becomes leader). If leader fails, he continues as It.
(Age, 6 up . . . Group, 5-20 . . . Time, 10 min.)

Scoot (also called "Ocean Wave"). Players are seated in strong chairs in circle with one vacant chair. When center player says, "Scoot right," all must protect chair to their right by scooting into it when it is vacant. On "Scoot left" they move to left. "It" tries to get into chair, and one responsible becomes It.
(Age, 6 up . . . Group, 8-30 . . . Time, 10 min.)

GAMES, STANDING OR WALKING

Bell Pass. Players stand in circle, hands behind them, and pass bell (or other noise maker) around behind their backs. It tries to guess who has bell, and when successful that person becomes It.
(Age, preschool up . . . Group, 10-30 . . . Time, 10 min.)

"I Say Stoop." Players stand in circle, leader in center. Leader says, "I say stoop!" and stoops, and all must do same. If he says, "I say stand," and stoops, all must remain motionless. Can be used on elimination basis, or just for fun.
(Age, 6 up . . . Group, 10-30 . . . Time, 10 min.)

Pass Left. Standing in circle, players are passing around two objects, several persons apart, trying to make rear one catch up with other. Leader calls, "Pass left" (if object is going to right), and they must shift. If any person gets both objects at same time, he is out, also if he happens to drop one. Or just play for fun.
(Age, 9 up . . . Group, 10-30 . . . Time, 10 min.)

Follow the Leader. Players are seated to start, but join him as he beckons. When he has several followers, they play "follow the leader," doing as he does. When signal is given, all rush for seats, and the one left out is leader. (Music could stop as signal, or leader could clap hands or shout "Go home.")
(Age, 6 up . . . Group, 10-50 . . . Time, 10 min.)

Opposite. Each player is holding handkerchief or corner of napkin, standing in circle. When leader calls, "Hold fast," all are to drop it. If he calls, "Drop it," they are to hold fast.

(Age, 9 up . . . Group, any size . . . Time, 5-10 min.)

Cracking Nuts. One or more "nuts" are in inside of circle formed by players, holding hands. The "crackers" are outside circle with rolled newspapers. Nuts are cracked by reaching over hands of circle and swatting them. When cracked, nut exchanges places with cracker. After a while, shift and get others in circle to become nuts or crackers.

(Age, 6 up . . . Group, 10-30 . . . Time, 10 min.)

Squirrel in the Tree. Players stand around room, two holding hands and a third in middle of their little circle, as the nut. There are two or more squirrels who are trying to get nuts. On signal called by squirrel, "Nuts," all must change trees, and each squirrel tries to get tree too. Those left out become chasers, and one or all will give signal, "Nuts!" for a change.

(Age, 6 up . . . Groups, 3 each . . . Time, 5-10 min.)

Swat the Fly. Players stand in close circle, hands behind them, extra It in center. One player starts passing swatter (rolled newspaper or soft bedroom slipper) around outside circle. When center person has back turned, some player slyly swats him and quickly passes swatter on. If caught, player goes to center to exchange places with It.

(Age, 6 up . . . Group, 10-30 . . . Time, 10 min.)

Electricity. Similar game except that shock (hand squeeze) is sent around circle constantly until It finally catches someone in the act.

(Age, 6 up . . . Group, 10-30 . . . Time, 10 min.)

Indoor Scavenger Hunt. Played in several groups (can be large) equidistant from leader, who is in center beside piano bench or table upon which "loot" may be placed. Each group chooses runner who will bring to leader whatever is called for. First one with correct object wins point for his team. Start simple and get harder. Sample objects:

Man's belt	Girl's anklet	Bobby pin
Girl's glove	Boy's undershirt	1928 Penny
Key ring	Black shoestring	Chip of nail polish

(Age, 9 up . . . Groups, 5-30 . . . Time, 10 min.)

Bird, Fish, Animal. Divided as in Indoor Scavenger Hunt, each team sends representative to center, who must return and act out bird, fish, or animal for his team. First team guessing by shouting out name gets a point. Send different runner each time.

(Age, 9 up . . . Groups, 5-30 . . . Time, 10 min.)

Run and Draw. Similar to Bird, Fish, Animal except that when person returns to his group, he must use pencil and paper to draw whatever he has been assigned, which might be simple like "catfish," or harder like "an automobile transmission," "a burned-out light bulb," "justice," or such words. No writing can take place. The person may nod or shake head to indicate "Yes" or "No."

(Age, 9 up . . . Groups, 5-30 . . . Time, 10 min.)

Shoe Scramble. All of one group remove shoes, place in center of floor. Those of other group mix them up and, at signal, scramble for proper shoes begins. Now repeat for opposite group. First one with own shoes on and laced up, wins. (If there are many shoes without laces, skip lacing.)
(Age, preschool up . . . Group, 5-100 . . . Time, 10 min.)

Feather Race. Who can blow his feather to finish line first?
(Age, preschool up . . . Group, 2 at least . . . Time, 10 min.)

Bean Bag Shuffle Board. Use sliding bean bags instead of pucks in shuffleboard.
(Age, 6 up . . . Group, 2-4 . . . Time, 10-60 min.)

Button Snap. Lanes 10 to 12″ wide are chalked on floor with a button in each. Object: all players start on signal, snapping by pressing edge of button, trying to get button to finish line first.
(Age, 6 up . . . Group, 5-10 . . . Time, 10 min.)

Candle Bowling. Arrange candles in lines of 1, 2, 3, and 4 as in bowling, near edge of table (with brown paper underneath to catch drippings). Stack books up so that player's chin is at right height to blow out candles. Each player gets two blows, as in bowling. If two tables are going, one can be used while other is being relighted. (Be careful of fire.)
(Age, 6 up . . . Group, 4-12 . . . Time, 10-45 min.)

Table Hockey. This ping-pong blow game can have four teams on rectangular table. Each is lined up at table's edge. One team starts blowing ping-pong ball to opposite table end. A point is counted against team for allowing ball to roll off their edge.
(Age, 6 up . . . Group, 8-24 . . . Time, 10-20 min.)

Group Ping-Pong. Players form circles at two ends of ping-pong table, one player holding paddle on each end of table. One serves, lays down paddle, other knocks it back, lays down paddle. Next person in line must pick up paddle and hit ball back. Can be elimination (out if you miss) or played just for fun. Sometimes single circle goes around entire table.
(Age, 6 up . . . Groups, 5-10 each . . . Time, 10-20 min.)

Ping-Pong Dodge Ball. Played as in regular dodge ball.

Chain Spelling. Two teams play. First team spells out name of word, and first player of other team must spell word in same category (such as cities, proper names, grocery items) beginning with last letter of first team's word before count of 10, or lose a point. First player might spell out NEW YORK. Whereupon first player of other team must spell KANSAS CITY (or some other beginning with K). May be played around table.
(Age, 9 up . . . Groups, 5-30 each . . . Time, 10-30 min.)

Dumb Crambo. There are two groups. One leaves room, other chooses verb, such as "eat." They send word to those outside that their verb rhymes with "heat." This team figures out answer, comes inside and acts it out. If it is right, players inside clap; if not, they shake their heads. Continue until hidden word is detected, then shift roles, inside team going outside, and new inside team choosing verb.

(Age, 9 up . . . Groups, 5-30 each . . . Time, 15-30 min.)

Occupational Wheel of Fortune. Large wheel with pointer is ready. It contains number of occupations. Player spins it until it stops and then acts out occupation for others to guess. (If group is divided into teams, he might return to his team and tell it, and have entire team act out occupation for others to guess.)
(Age 9 up . . . Group, any size; 1 player . . . Time, 10-30 min.)

Turtle Racing Game. Outlines of two or more turtles are cut from heavy cardboard, hole punched through head and strong string 20 feet or longer slipped through. String is tied to chair or table leg, just as high as turtle's length, so that his "hind legs" can touch floor. Hole in his head is large enough that animal slips on string easily.

At "Go" signal, all turtles start racing by having their masters start them on string from point farthest from chair leg. When master pulls or jiggles string and thus helps turtle's feet to touch the floor or ground, it can move up to goal. Some races have turtles go up and back.

This game may be made seasonal by using a cut-out appropriate for season, like Easter bunny, turkey, black cat, for Easter, Thanksgiving, Halloween, or it may be used as horse race.
(Age, 9 up . . . Group, 2-5 . . . Time, 10-30 min.)

CUMULATIVE GAMES

These are the games that keep adding on. Besides being fun, many of them are good memory drills.

Do This and Add Something. In circle of not more than 20 people, leader starts with action, such as tapping foot. Person to his right does leader's action, then adds one of his own, perhaps waving hand. Continue until all have done the action preceding, plus theirs. In group larger than 20, divide into at least two groups.
(Age, 6 up . . . Group, 8-20 . . . Time, 5-10 min.)

Aunt Sally Went Shopping. (May be done as performance stunt with five players who come up front, or in group of not more than 20.)

"My Aunt Sally went shopping and guess what she bought?" leader says. "What?" is answer. "A pencil sharpener." Whereupon each person must act it out, down the line, for his neighbor, and each action is continued for duration.

Other things she bought:

> Electric milker (milking motion)
> Some bubble gum (chewing)
> New bicycle (motion with feet)
> Spring seat (bounce up and down)
> Cuckoo clock (say, "Cuckoo, cuckoo")
> Spinning wheel (rock back and forth).

As large group activity, entire group begin to do action as soon as they are told or shown, making this suitable for auditorium and table use.
(Age, 6 up . . . Group, 5-20 . . . Time, 5-10 min.)

Auntie from Borneo. Using tune, "Bury Me Not on the Lone Prairie," leader sings first phrase, with group following in repetition, and so on through song. An action, once started, continues throughout.

Song: "My aunt came back from Borneo. The fan she brought goes to and fro." (Fan with right hand.) "My aunt came back from old Algiers. She brought to me a pair of shears." (Make cutting motion with first and second fingers of left hand.) "My aunt came back from Ararat. She brought to me a sailor hat." (Nod head.) "My aunt came back from Burma fair. She brought to me a rocking chair." (Add motion of rocking chair.) "My aunt came back from Kalamazoo. She brought to me, some gum to chew." (Chewing motion.)

(Age, 6 up . . . Group, any size . . . Time, 5-10 min.)

Ha Ha. With players seated in circle or around table, one player says, "Ha." Second one says, "Ha ha," and third, "Ha, ha, ha." Each one adds one more "Ha" than previous one did. No one must laugh. If so, extract a forfeit, have them drop out, or just start over and see who laughs least.

(Age, 9 up . . . Group, 8-20 . . . Time, 5 min.)

Quaker Meeting. Quakers are noted for their silence and solemnity. Groups in circle of not more than 20, preferably less. The leader solemnly taps person on his right on knee, lightly. Tap passes around circle. Than tap on cheek, or nose, or ear, or head goes around circle in same manner. No one must smile or laugh.

(Age, 9 up . . . Group, 8-20 . . . Time, 10 min.)

I'm Going to London . . . Seated around circle of up to 25 players, one player starts, saying "I'm going to London, and I'll take with me an apple." Next person adds something beginning with a "b" and so on. This is effective as game played when person from group is leaving for another town to work or live. Substitute that town for "London."

(Age, 6 up . . . Group, 8-25 . . . Time, 10 min.)

Count to 30. As players sit in circle, they try to count to 30, using certain rules. Instead of saying 7, 17, 27, etc. player places hands together, palms facing. Instead of saying any multiple of 7, put hands together, knuckles together, palms facing away from each other. Also, after any of these symbols has been given, the count reverses direction around circle, going back in other direction. If there is a miss, group starts over from some position across circle from where miss takes place. Trickiest combination is 27 (palms facing) and 28 (a multiple), with directions reversing at same time.

(Age, 9 up . . . Group, 8-30 . . . Time, 10-30 min.)

Buzz, Fizz. Same game as Count to 30 except that word, "buzz" is substituted for 7, 17, 27, and the like, and "fizz" for multiples. Reverse as above.

(Age, 9 up . . . Group, 8-30 . . . Time, 10-30 min.)

One Frog. Players seated in circle, one person leads, saying "One frog." Next person to his left says, "One head," next one, "Two eyes," next, "Four legs," next, "Petunk," and next "In the puddle." Then double each: "Two frogs," "Two heads," "Four eyes," "Eight legs," "Petunk, petunk," "In the puddle, in the puddle." Continue to see how high the group can get. After a miss, start over again.

(Age, 9 up . . . Group, 8-30 . . . Time, 5-10 min.)

Geography. One person in seated circle names geographical item: city, state, country, river, mountain; second person must give word beginning with last letter of first person's word. So on around circle. For missing: pay forfeit, drop out, or have mark chalked against you, whichever is agreed upon.

(Age, 9 up . . . Group, 8-30 . . . Time, 5-10 min.)

PASSING GAMES

In these games, players are seated in a circle, passing an object. Large groups can be divided into smaller circles, and the game can be played simultaneously in all the circles.

A What? There are several versions of this game. One is to start an object around circle to left saying, "This is a dog." Next person says, "A what?" Starter says, "A dog." Object is then passed to next person with same procedure, but "A what?" question is always relayed back to the starter, who in turn gives answer, which is relayed back around circle, gradually repeated a number of times. Simultaneously, with starting dog to left, he starts "cat" to right, with same procedure. A popular version is to have a several-word description, like "A freshly baked peach pie" and "A jar of watermelon pickles," or "This is a shawl with a long fringe" and "This is a pair of galoshes, slightly worn but wearable." (The longer the line, smaller the circle should be to enjoy it.) In any version, fun comes when the signals for dog and cat or others begin to cross each other halfway around circle, and players do not know which way to turn for "A what?"

(Age, 9 up . . . Group, 8-20 . . . Time, 10-15 min.)

Numbers Race. Two or more competing circles of same number of players are passing object around circle. Designate winning number of times object is to pass, such as six. Each time object goes by first person he counts aloud, "One," "Two," etc. After six complete revolutions, first one through, wins.

(Age, 9 up . . . Group, 8-20 . . . Time, 10 min.)

Pass It On. As music plays, an object is passed around circle, counter-clockwise. When music stops, whoever is caught must, next time he receives object, pass it under left leg, then pass it on. If caught second time, he adds: pass it around neck, then passes it on. If caught third time, adds: pass under right leg. For a fourth time adds: stand up. For a fifth, adds: sit down. (Also called "Musical Ball.")

(Age, 6 up . . . Group, 8-30 . . . Time, 5-10 min.)

Circle Poison. Similar game. If caught once, raise right hand. Twice, right hand and right leg. Three times, add: raise left leg. Four times: raise both hands, both legs, and then pass object past you.

(Age 6 up . . . Group, 8-30 . . . Time, 5-10 min.)

Musical Hats. As music plays, three hats are being passed around circle. Each person must try on hat, then pass it on, as it comes by him. When music stops, whoever has the hat on pays a forfeit, counts point against himself, or is eliminated.

(Age, 6 up . . . Group, 5-20 . . . Time, 5-15 min.)

Pass the Question. Folded piece of paper is passed around circle quickly. Whoever has it when music stops must answer question on slip. Then another question is passed around circle.

(Age, 9 up . . . Group, 5-30 . . . Time, 5-15 min.)

MYSTERY, PUZZLER, AND ACCOMPLICE GAMES

In these types of games, something is hidden. It may be a concrete object, or it may be a bit of information, a fact, a certain action, or a certain arrangement. The mind is challenged to solve the mystery or find the answer to the problem. In the following group of MYSTERY GAMES, It does not know the solution, but the group does—or sometimes It does know, and the group does not.

Who Am I? Each person has pinned on his back the name of a person. By asking questions that can be answered "Yes" or "No" he is to find out who he is.

(Age, 6 up . . . Group, 5-100 . . . Time, 10 min.)

Who Left the Room? While It is out of room, someone else leaves. It's job when he comes back is to figure out who left room.

(Age, 6 up . . . Group, 10-25 . . . Time, 10 min.)

I Have an Idea (also called Compliments and Slams). The group chooses an object while It is out of room. When he returns, player says, "I have an Idea." "How's that?" asks It. "Just like you," "How?" asks It, again. "Green," says player. (The object chosen was leaf on plant.) Here It may take one guess, then receive other clues. If he prefers, he does not have to guess, but never gets but one guess at a time. Continue until It has discovered the object. Person who gave last clue now goes out.

(Age, 9 up . . . Group, 10-50 . . . Time, 10-20 min.)

Teakettle. In this one, action is chosen, and when It returns to room, he uses the word, "Teakettle," instead of action, like "Would you teakettle alone?" Answers must be yes or no. Continue until the action is discovered.

(Age, 9 up . . . Group, 5-25 . . . Time, 10-20 min.)

Find the Leader. When It returns to room and goes to center of circle he finds people simultaneously doing same actions. His job is to find person who is leading them in what they are doing, for when any change comes, the leader must indicate it. When It catches leader, another person goes out.

(Age, 6 up . . . Group, 10-25 . . . Time, 10 min.)

How, When, Where. When It returns he finds that group has selected a noun, like the word, "trip." He asks any person three questions: "How do you like it?" "When do you like it?" "Where do you like it?" Answer might be, "Ever so much," "Whenever the opportunity presents itself," "Anywhere in the U. S. or abroad." Continue until It has guessed. Sometimes words with double meanings are chosen, like bear, bare.

(Age, 9 up . . . Group, 10-25 . . . Time, 10 min.)

Bronx Cheer, Organ Grinder Man, Magic Music, Clap Hot and Cold, Beat the Pan. These are all same basic game. When It returns from being out, something has been chosen for him to do, such as play piano. He is directed by these signals:

1. Clapping when he is going right, booing when he is going wrong.
2. Singing Organ Grinder Man, louder when he's close or ready to do it, softer when he's far away.
3. Playing piano or clapping and singing any song, louder and softer.
4. Clapping loud when he's close or hot, softer or very softly when he's far away.
5. Tin pan is beat upon, louder when close, softer when away. One person beats pan.

    (Age, preschool up . . . Group, 10-100 . . . Time, 10 min.)

Chain Reaction (Pantomime Gossip). While three persons are out or room, some action is figured out: changing a baby, washing an elephant, or taking down screens. One person is chosen to act this out for No. 1, who comes into room, and watches. Then No. 1 acts out what he thinks it is for No. 2, and No. 2 acts out what he thinks it is for No. 3. Then group tells them what was hidden action.

    (Age, 9 up . . . Group, 10-100 . . . Time, 15-20 min.)

Your Predicament. Group figures out predicament for person who is out. It has the privilege, on returning, of asking anybody in room what they would do in his place, which they must answer. If predicament were that he has date with two girls by mistake, answer might be, "I'd get sick," or "I'd try to reason with them."

    (Age, 12 up . . . Group, 10-25 . . . Time, 10-20 min.)

Pretzel (Chinese Puzzle).[10] If group is large, divide into smaller ones of ten who form circles. Each one sends one of its number out of room. Leader then helps those remaining to wind and twist, scramble, and so on without letting go their hands. Object: for person sent away to return and unscramble mess by telling which person will step over, duck under, twist, turn. No turning loose of hands!

    (Age, 9 up . . . Group, 10-25 . . . Time, 10-20 min.)

Statute. When It returns, he finds group all in poses. They are representing some famous person, and he is to guess who it is. Another way of playing would be for him to point to a player, who would go into his version of pose of that individual.

    (Age, 9 up . . . Group, 5-50 . . . Time, 10 min.)

Animal Crackers. Each person in group of 25 or less, has animal cracker, and is to describe animal, one clue at a time, to see if others can guess what his animal is.

    (Age, 6 up . . . Group, 5-25 . . . Time, 10 min.)

I'm Thinking of a Word. Player starts off in group of up to 50, seated in circle: "I'm thinking of a word that rhymes with light." Others must guess by acting out word, like "sight," "might." They say, "Is it . . . ?" then act out word they think it is. Whoever guesses correctly becomes It for next time.

    (Age, 6 up . . . Group, 5-100 . . . Time, 10 min.)

Imaginary I Spy (Dwarf Hide-and-Go-Seek). Player thinks of object in special location, such as the light overhead, and answers questions "Yes" or "No" from group until they discover where he has hidden it. Two may hide object at same time. Person who discovers where, becomes It.
(Age, preschool up . . . Group, any size . . . Time, 10 min.)

Twenty Questions. Same principle. Jim Flynn's automobile is thing Mary Alice Jones is thinking of, and he will answer questions (up to 20) "Yes" or "No." Sometimes played as "Vegetable-Animal-Mineral," and sometimes person who is It will reveal which of the three the object is. (House would be vegetable or mineral depending on whether it were wood or brick, in construction.) If group has not discovered in 20 questions, person who is It can try again, after telling them what object was.
(Age, 9 up . . . Group, 3-100 . . . Time, 10 min.)

Telephone Conversation. All participate in twos, each pair given five minutes to plan telephone conversation between two persons well known to group (either local folk or national or historical characters). Two designated to talk are indicated when leader hands them two toy telephones, or reasonably exact facsimiles. One person then goes across room and they talk back and forth. Object: for others to guess by their conversation who is being impersonated, on each end of "telephone." It could be such combinations as a TV character and a historical character from the past.
(Age, 9 up . . . Group, 5-50 . . . Time, 10-20 min.)

Running Indians. As group sits and waits, five members run through, single file, and out door. Then, in a minute, they run through again, in rearranged order. Object: to put them back in original order. This can be done by small groups observing, or as individuals. Indians may have Indian names on them for identification, especially in group who do not know each other very well—White Cloud, Running Deer, and the like.
(Age, 9 up . . . Group, 5-20 . . . Time, 10 min.)

Then here is a small group of PUZZLERS just as a sample of the many others that leaders can devise or find in other books.

Guess:

Number of beans, peas, or buttons in jar
Weight of dictionary in pounds and ounces
Length of ball of cord
Number of seeds in any kind of fruit
Number of words on page (magazine or newspaper)
Number of potatoes or apples in basket
(Age, 9 up . . . Group, any size)

Guess What. Hidden word or words are spelled out by articles displayed in order, like: SOUPY (soap, orange, union suit, peeling, yesterday's date).
(Age, 9 up . . . Group, any size)

Mystery Boxes. Several objects are in boxes of different sizes. People try to decide by rattle, sound and weight, what's in box.
(Age, 9 up . . . Group, any size)

Mystery Bags. In cloth bags (size of bean bag) insert articles, as above, and sew so that no one may see. Then let them feel to see if they can detect what hidden objects are. Number the bags.

(Age, 9 up . . . Group, 5-50)

Match Removal. Pair of players try by alternating withdrawals to force opponent to take last match. Matches are in three groups: 5, 4, 3. Up to all matches may be taken from any group at a turn, but not from more than one group at a turn. Toothpicks, sections of soda straws make good counters.

(Age, 9 up . . . Group, 2 . . . Time, 5-15 min.)

Sixteen Matches. In row are 16 matches. Two play. Players may pick up 1, 2, or 3 at a time. See who can make opponent take last match.

(Age, 9 up . . . Group, 2 . . . Time, 5-15 min.)

And finally there are ACCOMPLICE GAMES in which the leader and a partner are in cahoots, unknown to the other players. There is always a system and the point is for the group to figure out the system. It is customary to let anyone who thinks he knows the system try his luck.

Usually the group chooses some object to be indicated to the confederate by the leader.

Object Guessing. When confederate returns, he is to indicate chosen object which has been pointed to by leader. Objects are placed on chairs which are numbered, 1, 2, 3, 4, 5, left to right, by unwritten, unspoken understanding. If leader points to chair No. 1 first time, that would be correct one. Likewise, to point second to that on chair No. 2, point to No. 3, third. If he points to any other chair, that is, of course, not correct one.

(Age, 9 up . . . Group, 6-100 . . . Time, 10 min.)

Spoon Photography. While confederate is out of room, picture is taken with spoon as if by camera. Confederate names person "photographed", for leader is sitting in same posture as one whose picture was taken.

(Age, 9 up . . . Group, 6-50 . . . Time, 10 min.)

Turkey Gobbler. While accomplice is out of room, a small object, the turkey, is given to one of players, seated in circle on floor. Leader sits cross-legged, foot pointing to side of circle where turkey is hidden. As accomplice goes around listening to everybody's hands to hear turkey, he looks at leader, who wiggles toe slightly when he comes to right person. To make this seasonal, let hidden object be clock (New Year's), beating heart (Valentine's), firecracker (Fourth of July), music box (Christmas).

(Age, 9 up . . . Group, 6-50 . . . Time, 10 min.)

Name the Number. Group picks number, and when confederate returns to room, leader calls off: "44, 16, 10, 8, 6, 10." Accomplice says immediately, "32," which is correct. His clue: first numeral, 4, of the first number, tells him which numeral is significant, and second number, also 4, tells him what to multiply that fourth number by, giving him 4×8 or 32.

(Age, 12 up . . . Group, any size . . . Time, 10-30 min.)

Writing a Number with Matches. Actual number is number of fingers placed unobtrusively on edge of table after arranging matches (or toothpicks, pieces of soda straws) in geometric shapes. Each time you change number, change arrangement. Gradually make it more obvious until some catch on. You may have one or more accomplices who are in the know. After writing number with matches, tell group what number is.
(Age, 9 up . . . Group, 3-15 . . . Time, 10-30 min.)

Tom Thumb. When confederate returns to name chosen object from three, he finds leader giving him cue with hands—if right thumb is over left, it indicates article to right; if left is on top, to left; if both are parallel, to center.
(Age, 9 up . . . Group, 5-50 . . . Time, 10-15 min.)

Chopsticks. As leader crosses chopsticks in middle of room, confederate can tell which question will be the answer by noting that first stick is placed to represent 12 o'clock on clock face, and other will have head at o'clock hour which represents proper question, such as 4:00 o'clock, fourth question.
(Age, 9 up . . . Group, 5-50 . . . Time, 10 min.)

Number Guessing. When confederate leaves room, group chooses number from 1 to 156. After number is selected, leader places three coins on floor representing that number. Confederate is called back, he studies it, and gives number without hesitation. The key is face of clock, with dime representing center, nickel and quarter, the hour marking positions. Numeral on which quarter rests is squared (multiplied by itself), and numeral on which nickel rests is added or subtracted from squared number. (If nickel is head up, add; if tails up, subtract.)
(Age, 12 up . . . Group, 5-50 . . . Time, 10 min.)

Magic Writing (also called Mysterious Writing, Chinese Writing, Magic Cane). While confederate is out, group chooses word to be written to that person by leader. Word is transmitted by first letters of all sentences spoken by leader for consonants, and by tapping out vowels, one tap for A, two for E, three for I, four for O, and five for U. Color can be added by using dim lights, oriental tones, and mysterious motions that mean nothing with cane, yardstick, or wand, or flashlight, or magic rope.
(Age, 9 up . . . Group, 5-50 . . . Time, 10-15 min.)

Golly Golly. Variation of Magic Writing in that names of famous people are used and fingers denote vowels. Group chooses name of famous person and some associated phrase may be spelled out, for instance, Babe Ruth might be spelled "King of Swat."
(Age, 9 up . . . Group, 5-50 . . . Time, 10-15 min.)

Reading Temples. This can be very mysterious in appearance, and may be presented as hypnotism. When accomplice returns to room, having been sent out and a verb chosen, leader communicates to him in these ways:

1. Accomplice puts his hand on temples of leader, and leader says, "You must tell us the word." Then leader, by biting teeth together, gives signal, and accomplice counts. He bites 19-9-13-7 times, with pauses in between, to spell out word, "Sing." Muscles at temples flex every time leader bites, so it is easy to count.

2. Accomplice may be seated in chair and hypnotized by having leader pass soothing motions across his forehead. Really, he is spelling out, as above, word, with accomplice going through alphabet with him, as 19 strokes for S, 9 for I, 13 for N, and 7 for G. (A short-cut may be used by having extra long stroke to represent five counts. It may go from middle of forehead back to ears, where short stroke goes only to temples.) The hypnotized person then sings in dazed fashion, and many will believe in spell.

(Age, 9 up . . . Group, 5-100 . . . Time, 10-20 min.)

Legs. When accomplice returns, he can identify immediately object chosen by group in his absence, when questioned by leader, because it is next object mentioned by leader after something that has legs.

(Age, 9 up . . . Group, 10-50 . . . Time, 10-20 min.)

Which Panel? There are four panels on door. When leader calls accomplice back, he indicates which one by number of words he uses, like "Come on back in" for fourth panel.

(Age, 9 up . . . Group, 5-50 . . . Time, 10 min.)

Which Article? (Also called Jamboree.) Accomplice gets his signal as he leaves: leader unobtrusively puts fingers on door jamb to indicate which question in order, such as third, will contain correct answer. Group chooses article, and confederate says "No" until third question, or whatever one was indicated.

(Age, 9 up . . . Group, 5-50 . . . Time, 10 min.)

Nine Books. Confederate re-enters room to tell group which of nine books it chose, arranged in three rows of three, as in illustration.

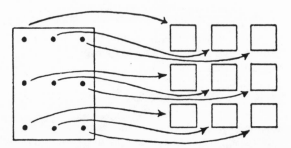

Leader touches spot on first book which indicates location of correct book.

(Age, 9 up . . . Group, 5-25 . . . Time, 10 min.)

Black Magic. Leader indicates chosen object to assistant by next thing pointed to after something black.

(Age, 9 up . . . Group, 5-50 . . . Time, 10 min.)

Red, White, Blue Magic. Same as black magic, but with more colors. Use in order on three different tries.

Power. All are sitting in circle and two persons move around in mystic manner making magic gestures. One asks other if he has the power yet. Trick comes when first person speaks after one of mystics says, "Power, power, power, come hither, power!" One mystic leaves room and other shakes hands with person who spoke. Naturally when the one who left returns, he can shake hands with same person.

(Age, 9 up . . . Group, 5-50 . . . Time, 10 min.)

In Cahoots. Same idea as Power. Accomplice places left hand on right shoulder of leader and follows around room while leader says, "The Magic Circle now begins" . . . and continues until some person speaks. Leader says to accomplice, "Are you in cahoots?" (meaning "Did you notice who spoke?") and he says, "Yes, I'm in cahoots," and leaves room. Then leader gives small object to person who spoke, and accomplice can, of course, come in and identify who has object. (If accomplice did not note who spoke, he says, "No, I'm not in cahoots.")

(Age, 9 up . . . Group, 5-25 . . . Time, 10 min.)

Time and Place. One individual goes out of room while group decides on city, hour, and minute. For example: Cincinnati, Ohio, 2:30 P.M. Partner, upon return of first person, recites list of cities and immediately is told by one who was out of room correct time and place. Technique is as follows: first, hour is given by name or names of cities in four time zones: Eastern time, 1, 2, 3; Central time, 4, 5, 6; Mountain time, 7, 8, 9; Pacific time 10, 11, 12. Person would say then, two cities in Eastern zone, e.g. Boston, Massachusetts and Philadelphia, Pennsylvania, and then shift to another time zone to give minutes. Letters with which next two cities begin designate minutes.

```
0 1 2 3 4 5 6 7 8 9
a b c d e f g h i j
```

Thus could be used Denver, Colorado, and Albany, New York. The next city designates either A.M. or P.M. Any city beginning with letters A-M stands for A.M. and between N and Z for P.M. For example: person might say Reno, Nevada. Name of city following any combination of three cities beginning with San or New is correct one.

When individual returns to room his partner could say, Boston, Massachusetts, Philadelphia, Pennsylvania, Denver, Colorado, Albany, New York, Reno, Nevada, New Haven, San Francisco, New York, Cincinnati, Des Moines and correct answer of 2:30 P.M. Cincinnati would be given immediately.

(Age, 12 up . . . Group, 3-25 . . . Time, 10-20 min.)

No, Nope. Accomplice leaves, object is selected by group, accomplice returns. Leader continues to point out wrong objects as long as reply is "Nope," but when accomplice shifts to "No" he means for leader next time to point to correct one, in which case he or she will say, "That's it."

(Age, 9 up . . . Group, 5-50 . . . Time, 10-20 min.)

Concentration. Accomplice leaves, and leader gets someone in group to write out sentence. Accomplice is to write same thing. Group writes, "Birds of a feather flock together." When accomplice returns, leader asks if he is ready. "Yes." "All concentrate, then, while he writes." They are supposed to be doing it. Accomplice writes out, "The same thing."

(Age, 9 up . . . Group, 5-100 . . . Time, 5 min.)

CREATIVE, IMPROVISING GAMES

In the following games, persons or groups are to improvise and then show what they have worked out. In some cases they will do it together. These games are different, a little more challenging.

Buckets. Seated in circle, group learns that each person is to pantomime bucket on floor in front of him. Each person, without talking and in turn, shows how high bucket is, what its other dimensions are, its shape, whether it has handle. After all have described their buckets in pantomime, they pantomime contents, then, one at a time, showing, by way they take it out, what it is (or way they let, say, "beans" run through their hands). Others may be asked to guess what is in bucket.

(Age, 9 up . . . Group, 8-15 . . . Time, 10 min.)

What's Wrong with This? In groups of 5 to 10, present stunt and let others figure out what is wrong in situation. This might be done in serious vein, like having someone committing a social error such as introducing man to woman.

It might be done in nonsense, like bride and groom skipping lively down aisle. (What's wrong? Groom is already married.) Three large people are trying to get under umbrella. (It isn't raining.)

Another angle: just simple turn-about, having characters dramatize unexpected, like youngster refusing cookies (might spoil his meal), wife saying that she didn't mind husband's being late for dinner—she knows he had some things to go over with his new secretary. What a pretty, intelligent girl . . ., and so on.

(Age, 9 up . . . Group, 5-10 . . . Time, 10 min.)

Concentration. In center of small circle stands individual whom all are touching. They are all looking toward one person in circle. If concentration is hard enough, center person will have tendency to fall toward person to whom all are looking!

(Age, 12 up . . . Group, 8-10 . . . Time, 5-10 min.)

Alibis. Leader tells of some incident that happened just before the meeting, gives exact time, and calls on different people to give their alibis as to where they were. (Pie was stolen from refreshment supply, for example.) Then have group vote on who was probably guilty.

(Age, 12 up . . . Group, 3-25 . . . Time, 15-25 min.)

Brainstorming. Business and industry are using this creative system, so why not for fun? In small groups of 3 to 10 persons, you simply take problem and think it through from all angles, sometimes coming up with some colossal ideas. One group took a few minutes to think up all the recreational things they could do, and were amazed that list totaled 75 items! Such subjects as "How could we raise some needed money?" or "What could we do for fun for next six months in our group?" might bring some truly workable answers. It's fun, too.

(Age, 12 up . . . Group, 3-10 . . . Time, 15-60 min.)

New Year's Resolutions (in April). Write out your resolutions, give them to member of group such as secretary, and open them about April 1 to see how well resolutions were kept.

(Age, 9 up . . . Groups, any size . . . Time, 10 min.)

Poetry Club. Select short piece of light poetry and make enough copies for each person to have one. Then number off in group until 10 or 12 people have numbers. They are, when their number is called, to stand and read their poetry in manner indicated:

1. A train announcer	6. With a stammer
2. Somebody without teeth	7. A forgetful fourth-grader
3. A small child	8. A Shakespearean actor-r-r
4. A first-class gossip	9. In old elocution style
5. With a lisp	10. As a mellow-voiced radio or TV announcer

(Age, 9 up . . . Group, 10-12 . . . Time, 15-20 min.)

Who's Who? Players sit in pairs, with chairs so arranged that you can see who are partners. Each player starts by exchanging names with his partner. Bob becomes Betty and Betty, Bob, for instance. Leader calls for two persons to change places, and he tries to get seat. Persons who change are not real ones, but ones currently carrying these names. If leader gets a seat, one left out becomes It, still bearing assumed name he or she had. Each time a person sits, he exchanges names with partner in other seat. At end, have several people do characterization of person whose name they had when game ended.

(Age, 12 up . . . Groups, 2 each . . . Time, 15-20 min.)

Putting Puns into a Sentence. Divide into groups and see who can make sentence containing most puns.

(Age, 12 up . . . Groups, 3-5 . . . Time, 10-20 min.)

Creative Writing. Divide into groups and let each one try its hand at writing ads, singing commercials, composing grace for table, writing limerick or serious piece of poetry. Display works of art or have them read.

(Age, 12 up . . . Groups, 2-5 each . . . Time, 10-30 min.)

FUN WITH ART MATERIALS

Paper, paints, crayons, finger paints, water colors, and the like can furnish many enjoyable hours both for children and for youth and adults. Many of these activities, very informal in the arts and crafts line, can be done with little advance preparation. Some can be used for early comers at parties.

Making Name Tag. At affairs where this is needed, name tags may be made from slips of paper or cardboard, decorated gaily with crayolas, wax pencils. It is important that name can be read for some distance away. Have table (or several tables for large crowd) at which each may take some time to make his own. Wooden name tags are popular. They may be decorated with wax pencils, with new ball-point decorators' colors, or by wood-burning needles. Colorful yarn, used through holes, makes it easy to hang this one around neck. By distributing yarn carefully, groups may be formed automatically by color of yarn.

(Age, 6 up . . . Group, 1 . . . Time, 10-20 min.)

Self-Expression. As people arrive at party, have some art tables equipped with materials: paper hat materials, paper sack puppet materials, sculpture with apples, pears, or potatoes, or soap or modeling clay. "See what you can do" may be followed by "See what I made."
(Age, 6 up . . . Group, 1 . . . Time, 15-30 min.)

Art Exhibit. Divide into groups of 3 to 6 persons, give them scissors, paper, crayons, pins, and have them make children's cutouts, to be displayed later.
(Age, preschool up . . . Groups, 3-6 each . . . Time, 15-60 min.)

Silhouettes. Get early comers to have their silhouettes made. Put sheets of paper on wall and have someone shine a bright light close enough to his profile to cast shadow on paper. Outline with crayon or charcoal. Display.
(Age, 9 up . . . Group, 1 . . . Time, 15-25 min.)

Making Own Favors, Place Cards. With materials, such as paste, scissors, construction paper, feathers, cork, felt, raisins, marshmallows, each person is given opportunity to make his own favor or place card. Or make place cards or favors for another person. (Here is opportunity to make something nice for older person or bedridden individual.)
(Age, preschool up . . . Group, 1 . . . Time, 10-30 min.)

Abstractions and Concretions. Use sheet of pastel-colored paper and box of crayons (24-color box is good). First person uses one color and draws any line or enclosure, avoiding making it look too much like any object. Next person takes a color and draws an addition. Change colors when changing turns. Result is interesting for any age, any situation. Good family game.
(Age, 12 up . . . Group, 1 . . . Time, 10-60 min.)

Colors. Have enough sets and jars of paints for all to try their hand at a paint job, either to do as just for fun or to make Christmas card, favors, and the like.
(Age, preschool up . . . Group, 1 . . . Time, 10-60 min.)

Paper Fashions. Divide into small groups, each electing girl as model. Boys or men in group must design and make costume with newspapers, pins, scissors. Girls may advise but not help.
(Age, 9 up . . . Group, 5-15 . . . Time, 15-25 min.)

Blindfolded Drawing. Each person trying is blindfolded and led to his sheet of paper on wall (or blackboard). There he draws some object as directed (animal, landscape, person).
(Age, 6 up . . . Group, 1 . . . Time, 15-25 min.)

Self-Portrait. With paper bag on his head, each person draws, with crayon, eyes, one at a time, ears, nose, mouth, eyebrow, cheeks.
(Age, preschool up . . . Group, 1 . . . Time, 5-20 min.)

Pinhole Pictures. Each person has several grains of rice to drop on his drawing sheet. He punches hole in paper with pin where each grain lay, then draws picture including all these points.
(Age, 6 up . . . Group, 1 . . . Time, 5-15 min.)

Star Tracing. Duplicate number of double stars, outer of which is about 6 inches from point to point, and inner one an inch smaller, tip to tip, as illustrated. Place mirror about an inch from point of star. Object is to try to trace within lines of double star, between

Star Tracing

inner and outer stars. Several mirrors permit several star tracings to go on at same time. Excellent as guests arrive at party.

(Age, 9 up . . . Group, 1 . . . Time, 5-15 min.)

Doodles

1. Give everyone slips of paper and pencil (or crayons) and encourage them to doodle. Pass doodles around table, display them on wall, perhaps judge them for best.
2. Another version is best as blackboard game, in sight of all. One person starts by drawing line of some sort, perhaps irregular or wavy, on board. Whoever has an idea may come forward, take chalk, complete it into picture, then erase and start another doodle.

(Age, 9 up . . . Group, 1 . . . Time, 5-15 min.)

Blot Drawing. Each person makes ink blot on his paper, folding it while ink is still wet, then completes it into picture as directed by leader: cow, plane, Superman, bird, person. Display results.

(Age, 9 up . . . Group, 1 . . . Time, 5-15 min.)

Drawing in the Dark. Each person has paper and pencil (or crayons) and large sheet of paper. Explain that since so many are bashful about drawing when people are looking, you are having them draw in the dark. Give assignment and tell in order what parts to draw, like a house, then windows, then chimney, smoke coming from chimney.

(Age, 6 up . . . Group, 1 . . . Time, 5-10 min.)

Illustrated Music. As tunes are played on piano, one or more illustrators work at blackboard to draw appropriate pictures for titles, such as "Home on the Range." May be contest with two or more drawing.

(Age, 9 up . . . Group, any size . . . Time, 20-30 min.)

Editing a Paper. Dividing larger crowd into smaller groups, each is given assignment in editing paper, like sports, household hints, society, comics, want ads, front page, editorials, and the like. After 15 to 30 minutes, each presents its version of the news.
(Age, 9 up . . . Groups, 3-8 each . . . Time, 30-40 min.)

Magazine Autobiography. Provide materials, scissors, paste, notebook paper and cover, magazines, for each person to make up tongue-in-cheek notebook, "The Life and Works of _____," to be shown to others after 30 to 45 minutes of preparation. Angles might be: "First Photo," "Childhood," "Aim in Life," "Greatest Enjoyment," "Biggest Mistake," "Best Friend," "My Travels," "My Hobby," "My Finish." All illustrations are to be clipped from magazines.
(Age, 9 up . . . Group, 3-8 . . . Time, 30-40 min.)

Mother Goose Commercial. In small groups, redo Mother Goose in manner of today's commercials, including singing.
(Age, 6 up . . . Group, 2-8 . . . Time, 30 min.)

Snow Modeling (winter game). Provide dishpan of clean snow for each small group from which they are to model some interesting figures and display them, in about 15 to 20 minutes.
(Age, 6 up . . . Group, 3-5 . . . Time, 15-20 min.)

What Is It? Arrange on several tables odds and ends: needles, pins, corks, cotton, glue, nuts, prunes, pickles, pine cones. On center table are three resting places: pan with sawdust, bird cage, and bowl of water. People are to make strange creatures with these materials and display them. They are then placed in proper place, whether bird, beast or fish, for others to see.
(Age, 6 up . . . Group, 1 . . . Time, 15-30 min.)

Confetti Pictures. Have enough paste and confetti for each person to make a futuristic picture. Display them, with appropriate names.
(Age, 6 up . . . Group, 1 . . . Time, 15-30 min.)

Thread Sketching. Each person gets piece of white cloth and plenty of black thread. Idea is to sketch interesting picture with black thread. Scissors are available in case of error. Finished products are displayed gallery style. Some might be cartoons, some landscapes.
(Age, 6 up . . . Group, 1 . . . Time, 15-30 min.)

Make a Hat. Seasonal party idea. With colored paper, cloth, scissors, pins, and ornaments, either have small team make hat for one of its members, or have everybody make one, appropriate for party theme.
(Age, 6 up . . . Group, 1 . . . Time, 15-30 min.)

MAGAZINE GAMES

With scissors, paste, and imagination, individuals and groups can have a lot of fun with old magazines. Children can cut and paste into scrapbooks those things which interest them. Adults often enjoy doing this, too. Here are some other suggestions for the use of magazines that are partylike.

Scavenger Hunt. As in regular scavenger hunt, each group is given list of things to hunt for, to be found in perhaps 10 or 15 minutes. Whoever has most nearly complete list, wins. (Divide larger group down into groups of three or four each.)

Story. Each group is given magazine, and is to write story, using clippings from features, stories, ads, or anything else found in magazine. (Done in groups of three or four.)

Love Letters. See who can take their magazine and compose with clippings and explanations a good, mushy love letter. (Groups of three or four.)

Other Letters. Same idea as Love Letters, but letters to the President, to an enemy, to Santa, to St. Valentine, to Uncle Sam, to a Witch, and others.

Magazine Covers. Let small groups work with water colors, paper, crayons, scissors, paste, and other materials to create magazine cover. Alternate: to pose in tableau form, a magazine cover.

Magazine Costumes. Find costume in magazine, then dress one of members of group in that style, using sheets from magazine.

Make Up Your Own. Give out magazines to small groups and let them make up their own magazine game.
(Age, 9 up . . . Group, 2-6 . . . Time, 15-30 min.)

BLINDFOLD GAMES

Blindman's Buff. Players circle around blindfolded blind man, singing verse of a song. They stop at end. The blind man points stick at someone in circle and asks him to bark like a dog, or use his voice in some other way. The player does so, disguising voice. If blind man can still detect who it was, they change places.
(Age, preschool up . . . Group, 8-50 . . . Time, 10 min.)

Bell Tag. All players are blindfolded except bellboy (or girl), who rings bell as he or she moves around. Others try to catch her or him. If successful, they change places.
(Age, preschool up . . . Group, 5-40 . . . Time, 10 min.)

Tight Rope Walker (Blindfolded). Stretch rope on floor, and one at a time blindfold contestants and let them see who can walk farthest on rope.
(Age, 6 up . . . Group, 1 at a time . . . Time, 10 min.)

Pillow Fight (Blindfolded). Each of two blindfolded persons is given pillow, with instructions to hit the other. They are started from opposite ends of room. Unknown to them, third person has a pillow, and pelts them before they get to each other. He goes from one to the other.
(Age, 6 up . . . Group, 2 . . . Time, 10 min.)

Pickup. Blindfold a person, get him to pick up handful of coins or other objects that have been dropped to floor.

(Age, 9 up . . . Group, 1 . . . Time, 10 min.)

Blindfold Walk. Blindfold several players and send them across room. Idea is not to (1) ring any of bells that are hung from ceiling, (2) step on egg shells that are on floor, (3) bump into furniture that is in the way.

(Sometimes these things will be removed, and those watching will get delight from seeing contestants try to dodge what is not there.)

(Age, 6 up . . . Group, 5-10 . . . Time, 10 min.)

Blindfold Fortunes. Certain things are symbolic of fortunes. Load up table with number of these things, have blindfolded players walk up one at a time and place finger down on object. This automatically tells fortune, for example:

coins (for wealth)   toy plane (tape a trip)
ring (for marriage)   pile of dirt (farming)
dolls (for number of children)   top (spinster)

(Age, 6 up . . . Group, any size . . . Time, 15-20 min.)

BALLOON GAMES

Besides lending color and gaiety to any party, there are many games that can be played with balloons—in fact, just about all the games for which you would ordinarily use a ball.

Balloon Dart. Fill balloons with gas, tie them to furniture or other anchors so that they float. Give players darts and have them throw darts in turn, to puncture balloons. All players stay behind same line; darts are dangerous.

Hot Air. Give each person balloon. With all starting at same time, see who can blow his balloon up to bursting point first. Or, do it in pairs, and continue as elimination contest (loser drops out).

Balloon Defense. Have group choose partners and tie balloons to the ankles of one of each pair. The partners, working together, try to defend the balloon from being stepped on, but to burst others' balloons at same time. (Can be played singly.)

Balloon Relays

1. Each person kicks balloon up to line or goal, then breaks it by stamping on it.
2. Each person bats balloon with paddle to goal, then breaks it by hugging it.
3. Each person runs to goal with balloon between knees, then sits down on balloon on chair at goal to break it before returning.
4. Each person blows balloon to goal line, then sits on it to break it before returning.

5. Pass small balloon under chin down the line to end of relay line. First one through, wins. (If one breaks, head person must blow up and start another balloon.)
6. Seated in long line, each player must run around head of his line, back to his seat, blow up his balloon and sit on it to burst it, before next player down line from him can run. Several lines of equal numbers are competing.

Balloon Sweep. Each team of five or six has balloon, some spares, and broom, and its members stand in circle. At signal, first player with broom sweeps balloon around circle and back to place, then next one does same. If team breaks balloon it must blow up another and tie it.

Balloon Squeeze. Two or more pairs are competing. They blow up balloon, tie it or hold it, put it between them, and squeeze until it breaks. (Could be used as relay of pairs.)
(Age, 18 up . . . Groups, 2 each . . . Time, 5-10 min.)

Wastebasket Basketball. Played like regular basketball, except that there is no dribbling (balloon is passed or batted) and that goal is wastebasket, carried by team member, who must stand in place but can bend around to help ball in. Devise your own rules.
(Age, 9 up . . . Group, 4-10 each . . . Time, 10-20 min.)

Creative Activity with Balloons. Divide large group into several small ones, 3 to 6 persons. Give each group eight or ten balloons and some scotch tape. Let group make something to be shown to other groups in about 15 minutes. Animals are usually made, but try other things, too. Let preschool children try it.

Balloon Tail. Each person has balloon either under belt, fastened on back, or tied to string around waist and hanging down in back. Object: to protect your balloon tail but at same time to break other balloons.
(Age, 6 up . . . Group, any size . . . Time, 5-10 min.)

Balloon Hockey. Opposite wall is designated as goal for team. Play with two teams, each person equipped with cardboard fan to fan or bat balloon. Object: to knock balloons so as to hit goal of other team and make point. One or several may be put into play at midfield at same time. One team may knock red balloons, other team blue.

Balloon Volleyball. Players are sitting in chairs with string stretched between as net. Outside lines are indicated, as in volleyball. No player may get up out of seat; otherwise play as in regular volleyball. Object: to score point by knocking balloon in such manner that it touches floor on opponent's side, inside line. Set your own total point score for winning.
(Age, 9 up . . . Groups, 4-10 . . . Time, 10-20 min.)

Balloon Dodge Ball. In fairly small circles (so that balloon can actually be thrown at players) play dodge ball with balloons.
(Age, 6 up . . . Groups, 8-15 . . . Time, 5-10 min.)

Balloon Basketball. Five players are sitting in chairs in two lines facing each other, with goalie sitting in chair at end of setup. Lines are close enough that feet of opposing players may touch. Each team will bat balloon to its own right to its human goalie, who is holding his arms in circle. Goalie may bend or contort in any way except leave chair. No other player may leave chair. The game is started by having a referee toss balloon into air in middle of two lines. Successful goal is two points. Set time limit in beginning, such as 6 or 10 minutes. Substitutions may be used. Cheers from sidelines may be organized, and teams even named. May be played at cleared table, with 4 to 5 players on side and goalie at each end, with referee for each table.

(Age, 9 up . . . Groups, 4-6 each . . . Time, 10-30 min.)

Balloon Headball. A string as net is tied about 5½ feet high, and players play on both side of net in teams. Serving is by hitting ball over net with head, and playing as in volleyball. It is a foul to hit ball with hands, although you might permit hitting with shoulders, if agreed in advance. String may be raised or lowered, depending on ability of players.

(Age, 6 up . . . Groups, 5-10 each . . . Time, 10 min.)

FORFEITS OR CONSEQUENCES

A number of games call for the possibility of forfeits. Generally they are simple individual stunts which could be done without idea of forfeit for group amusement.

Imitations

1. Three barnyard noises
2. Jack-in-the-box
3. Monkey eating bananas
4. A back-seat driver
5. A ballet dancer in action
6. A mule braying
7. An opera singer
8. A child giving first recitation
9. A tightrope walker
10. An organ grinder's monkey
11. An umpire
12. Three bird calls
13. A photographer taking pictures
14. Paul Revere
15. A shadow boxer
16. A radio or TV announcer
17. A dog chasing a cat
18. Imitate a cat chased by a dog
19. A TV comedian, tell who it is
20. A Western hero's horse
21. Someone taking a shower
22. A politician, warming up
23. A trick dog
24. A soap salesman selling new soap
25. A Hollywood producer
26. A truant officer, going after someone present
27. A barker at a circus or carnival
28. Two Shakespeare or Dickens characters
29. Some unknown celebrity (Let group guess who you are.)
30. The Statue of Liberty

Speeches

1. Three nice compliments about yourself
2. The political situation
3. The plight of the farmer
4. Flowery compliments to three persons present
5. A funny story
6. A Mother Goose rhyme
7. A speech without words, only lip movements
8. The three books you would want to take with you to a desert island
9. The three big shots you'd like to know most
10. Your pet peeve
11. An exploit to brag about

12. Counting as far as you can in a breath
13. Your funniest joke—without smiling
14. Why you like your hobby
15. Answer truthfully two questions put to you
16. Where you'd like to spend your vacation and why
17. Reciting "Mary Had a Little Lamb"
18. Reciting anything you know from Shakespeare
19. Giving this yell twice: Owha tagoo Siam

Actions

1. Laugh, cry, whistle and sing in four corners of the room.
2. Kneel to three persons, smiling as you do it.
3. Hop like a grasshopper.
4. Yawn until somebody else does.
5. Do some acrobatic act.
6. March like a tin soldier.
7. Whirl around with an imaginary partner.
8. Dance a jig.
9. Crawl across the floor.
10. Sing like a popular male star; or female star.
11. Give a hen's triumphant cry that she's laid an egg.
12. Give the rooster's claim for part credit.
13. Leave the room with two legs, come back with six (a chair or small table).

Heavy, Heavy Hangs Over Thy Head. If forfeits are used as such, an article is demanded from each person losing out in game. (Sometimes game is made hard to get forfeit item from everyone.) There is a judge, over whose head article is hung (without his seeing it). "Heavy, heavy hangs over thy head," says official. "Fine or superfine?" asks judge. "Fine," says helper, meaning that it is boy's item. Whereupon judge pronounces what is to be done. (The preceding lists would be of help in prompting his imagination. However, it is easy to make forfeits seasonal. For New Year's, speech on My Resolutions; for Valentine's, on Love; for Halloween, on Witches.)

Color Forfeits or Stunts. During refreshments, pass around candies of different colors, and get one or more persons for each color to do stunt.

Stir the Broth. First player says, "I will stir the broth if (name of someone present) will recite the Gettysburg Address." If he won't, he must stir the broth. (You may actually have some broth to stir.) Person stirring does not stop until he finds someone who will *not* do as requested.

    (Age, 9 up . . . Group, 1 at a time . . . Time, 10-20 min.)

NOVEL OR QUIET RELAYS AND RACES

Many of these relays can be performed in circles instead of lines, particularly those which involve passing an article. This enables everyone to see how his team is doing and enjoy the actions of his teammates. When a team has completed its action everyone yells or stands up. These relays were collected by Bert Lyle.

Crazee Man Walk (Age: 10 up)

EQUIPMENT: Each team provided with potato (or orange or ball) and book. FORMATION: Teams in file formation; turning point, 15 feet in front of each team. DIRECTIONS: First player puts potato between his knees and book on his head. Without using his hands he moves to turning point and back, tagging second man. Action is repeated until all finish. Peculiar waddling gait attained by performers is great cause of merriment. Sometimes chain is added which has to be twirled on right index finger.

Orange Passing (Age: 8 up)

EQUIPMENT: Orange, apple, ball, or grapefruit for each team. FORMATION: Teams in file or circle formation. DIRECTIONS: On signal to start, first player puts orange under his chin, and without using his hands passes it to second player who takes it with his chin, and without use of his hands. Orange is passed down line in this manner. If dropped, can be retrieved by hand, but must be passed on by person dropping it. First team to complete passing, wins.

Raisin Relay (Age: 8 up)

EQUIPMENT: Saucer of raisins for each team and toothpick for each player. FORMATION: Teams in file or circle formation. First player in each team has saucer of raisins, and each player has toothpick. DIRECTIONS: On signal, leader spears three raisins on his toothpick and feeds them to next person in line. Leader then passes saucer to second person who spears three raisins and feeds them to third in line. Continue until all are finished.

Hand Clasp Relay (Age: 8 up)

EQUIPMENT: From three to six peanuts (or marbles or stones) for each team.

FORMATION: Teams in file or circle formation. Each player grasps his teammate's right wrist with his left hand. The peanuts are placed on desk or chair in front of first player.

DIRECTIONS: At signal, first player picks up peanuts, one at a time, and passes them down line as rapidly as possible; last player puts them on chair beside him. In similar manner, peanuts are then passed back up lines so that they will be in their original positions at end of game. If peanut is dropped, it must be picked up without unclasping hands. Team that first passes all peanuts down and back, wins relay.

VARIATION: Instead of clasping wrists, place hands palm to palm, interlacing fingers.

Tennis Ball Relay (Age: 10 up)

EQUIPMENT: Tennis ball, orange, or apple for each team.

FORMATION: Teams divided into pairs according to height. Pop bottle for each team is placed on table corner or small stand.

DIRECTIONS: First pair faces each other and place both hands on each other's shoulders. Tennis ball is placed between two foreheads and held there without using hands while pair walks to pop bottle and gently balances ball on small end of bottle. As soon as ball is resting securely they grab ball and run with it to next couple in line. If ball is dropped, pair dropping it must start over again from beginning line.

Kick the Stick Relay (Age: 6 up)

EQUIPMENT: Crooked stick about 12 inches long for each team.

FORMATION: Teams in file formation with stick in front of each team.

DIRECTIONS: First player kicks stick to turning point and back, leaving it in front of next player, who repeats action. Sticks are to be pushed along ground, not kicked up into air. Line finishing first is winner.

Egg Relay (Age: 12 up)

EQUIPMENT: One egg for each team; tablespoon for each player.

FORMATION: Teams in circle or file formation. Good table game. Each member holds tablespoon in his mouth.

DIRECTIONS: Object is to pass egg down line by tilting head with spoon in mouth. (Boil eggs, but don't let players know it.)

Post Card March Relay Age: 10 up

EQUIPMENT: Post card, alphabet card, or calling card for each team.

FORMATION: Team in file formation.

DIRECTIONS: First player puts post card between his nose and upper lip and marches to turning point and back. He exchanges card with second player without using hands, and action is continued until all have finished.

Clodhopper Race (Age: 10 up)

EQUIPMENT: Dozen or so little pieces of paper for each team.

FORMATION: One player from each team, preferably one with biggest feet, is chosen and blindfolded. Rest of team forms circle and scatters pieces of paper on floor.

DIRECTIONS: On signal to start, blindfolded players must try to step on each piece of paper in his circle. He is directed by his group only in what they say to him. They cannot touch him, or move themselves. First one to step on every single piece of paper is winner.

Gossip Relay (Age: 8 up)

FORMATION: Teams in file or circle formation.

DIRECTIONS: Sentence is whispered to first player of each team, and he whispers it to next person in line, who passes it to next. So it goes on to last players, who run to leader and tell what they heard. The team finishing first with most correct message wins, but final messages are usually more entertaining than competition among the teams.

Gobble Relay (Age: 10 up)

EQUIPMENT: Each team is provided with box or basket containing number of edible items wrapped in waxed paper—one for each member of team.

FORMATION: Table with baskets of food is equidistant from all teams. Chair is placed next to each team's basket.

DIRECTIONS: At signal, first member rushes to table, picks up article of food, sits in chair, raises feet off ground, unwraps package, eats food, says "Thank you," and returns to his team. This is continued until all have eaten. Contestant must keep feet off floor while eating. Half fun is in watching hesitation in choosing of packages. Good food items are apples, crackers, gumdrops, popcorn, taffy.

Stepping Stone Relay (Age: 11 up)

EQUIPMENT: Two bricks, or similar objects, for each team.

FORMATION: Teams in single file.

DIRECTIONS: First man in each line puts one brick out, steps on it, puts other down, and steps on it. Then he reaches back, gets first, and places it ahead of him. Thus, he continues across course and back. Second man walks on bricks same way; and gives to number three. This continues until all are through.

VARIATIONS: Use folded newspaper, footstools, chairs, or boxes.

Pushing Peanuts (Ping-pong balls) (Age: 8 up)

EQUIPMENT: Peanuts or ping-pong balls.
FORMATION: Players line up on hands and knees.
DIRECTIONS: Players push peanuts with their noses.
VARIATIONS: Use toothpick or pencil held in teeth to push peanuts. Potatoes may sometimes be used for peanuts.

Hobble Relay (Age: 10 up)

EQUIPMENT: Rubber band cut from inner tube, about four inches long for each team.
FORMATION: Teams in file formation. Turning point in front of each team.
DIRECTIONS: At signal, first player in each line slips rubber band over both feet up to ankles. He then hobbles to goal and returns, giving band to next player, and so on. Players must walk; they cannot jump or work band up on legs. Peculiar waddle motion is laugh provoker for other players and audience.

Suitcase Race (Age: 12 up)

EQUIPMENT: Each contestant has suitcase and umbrella. In suitcase are hat, coat, gloves, and any other clothing desired; contents should, however, be uniform.
DIRECTIONS: At signal, all contestants run to goal, open suitcases, put on clothes, close suitcases, open umbrellas, and run to starting point.

Match Box Relay (Age: 10 up)

EQUIPMENT: Covers off penny boxes of matches.
FORMATION: File formation or circle.
DIRECTIONS: Place match box cover over end of first player's nose. On "go" he "passes" box to nose of second player without using hands. When dropped, box may be picked up, however. Continue down line until every person's nose has been fitted.

Cracker Whistle Race (Age: 8 up)

EQUIPMENT: Ordinary soda crackers (or any type cracker).
FORMATION: Two teams of equal number in parallel lines facing each other.
DIRECTIONS: Each player has cracker. First players eat crackers, and as soon as they finish eating they whistle. As soon as they whistle, second players begin. Player cannot begin until after preceding player has whistled.

Penny Push (Age: 8 up)

EQUIPMENT: Yardstick, two chairs (or other level supports for yardstick), toothpicks (or soda straws) for each person, and one penny for each team. (Each team has yardstick, chairs.)

FORMATION: File formation.

DIRECTIONS: Split groups so that one person can push penny up yardstick, and another person pushes it back. Pennies are pushed with straw or toothpick clenched in teeth. Continue until all have finished.

Soda Straw and Bean Contest (Age: 9 up)

EQUIPMENT: Soda straw for each player and one container full of beans.

FORMATION: File or circle formation.

DIRECTIONS: Place beans in one container. Suck on soda straw and try to move beans one at a time to empty container.

Eggshell Relay (Age: 10 up)

EQUIPMENT: Eggshell with its contents removed (or a ping-pong ball) for each team. Also a fan or 10 × 12-inch cutout of stiff cardboard for each team.

FORMATION: Each team in file facing turning point some 20 feet away. This turning point can be soda bottle, rock, book, or any other object indicated.

DIRECTIONS: First player of team puts eggshell on ground and begins to fan it with his fan. He drives it around turning point and returns to his starting position. He then hands fan to second player who repeats procedures. This is continued until last man finishes. Players are not permitted to kick or touch eggshell in any way.

Candle Blow and Light Relay (Age: 9 up)

EQUIPMENT: Candle and matches.

FORMATION: File.

DIRECTIONS: First runner goes to candle, strikes match and lights candle, then runs back and touches second runner. Second runner blows out candle, relights it and returns to teammates. This continues until all the team have completed their turn.

Candle Race (Age: 9 up)

EQUIPMENT: Candle and matches.

FORMATION: File.

DIRECTIONS: First runner of each team lights candle, carries it to touch point, and returns to home base where he gives it to next runner. If candle goes out, runner must return home, light candle and repeat course. First team having all runners finish course, wins.

VARIATION: Use this as shuttle relay.

Apple Race (Book) (Age: 9 up)

EQUIPMENT: Apple, book, or similar object for each team.

FORMATION: File formation with touch line 20 feet away.

DIRECTIONS: First player puts apple on head and walks to touch line and back to starting line. He then gives apple to second player, and so on down line. If apple is dropped, it must be picked up and placed back on head.

Writing or Drawing Relay (Age: 10 up)

EQUIPMENT: Chalkboard and chalk for each team.
FORMATION: Players of each team in single file.
DIRECTIONS: First player runs to chalkboard and writes word on board. Each player continues this action. Object is to have completed, readable sentence after last player has finished. Correctness and speed are both required in this relay.
VARIATION: Each player draws line, attempting to create picture. Sometimes two turns are allowed in order for picture to be completed.

Pillowcase Relay (Age: 9 up)

EQUIPMENT: Pillow and case for each team.
FORMATION: Members of each team lined up, single file.
DIRECTIONS: On signal, first player takes pillow out of case and then puts it back. He passes it to second player who does same. First line through, wins.

Baby Bottle Race (Age: 12 up)

EQUIPMENT: Baby bottle of milk with new, enlarged hole, nipple for each person.
FORMATION: Each team in single file.
DIRECTIONS: Contestant kneels, with hands behind him while teammate holds bottle. Put only a little milk in each bottle. Contestants run in turn to chair, where bottle is held, put on fresh nipple, suck bottle, return to line, and tag teammate.

"Pop" Races (Balloons or Paper Sacks) (Age: 10 up)

EQUIPMENT: Balloon or paper sack for each person; chair for each team.
FORMATION: Each team in single file.
DIRECTIONS: First man runs to chair 20 feet from home, blows balloon or sack, and pops it by sitting on it. He then runs back and tags next man. Bags must be popped before leaving chair.
VARIATION: Have each team seated in chairs or on ground. First player runs around chair and back to place, blows up balloon or sack, and then sits on it. Second player can't start until balloon is popped.

Alphabet Relay (No: 12-10, Age: 12 up)

EQUIPMENT: Set of cards for each team.
FORMATION: Teams grouped equidistant from spelling area.
DIRECTIONS: Each player has one or more cards. Words are called out by leader, and players with appropriate letters dash into position at other end of

room to form word. First team finishing, gets a point. Double letters are represented by swinging card from side to side.

VARIATIONS: Call word, teams spell it out backwards

Split Affinities: Leader calls out affinities omitting last word. Players dash into place to spell it out.

EXAMPLES:

Adam & _____ (Eve)
Alpha & _____ (Omega)
Fair & _____ (Warmer)
Bread & _____ (Butter)
Half & _____ (Half)
Soap & _____ (Water)
Thunder & _____ (Lightening)
Assault & _____ (Battery)

Numbers Racket (No: 20-60, Age: 12 up)

EQUIPMENT: Use cards about 4 × 6 inches with numbers up to 25, or for smaller groups just to 10.

FORMATION: Teams with each player holding number card.

DIRECTIONS: Leader calls out number. Since each team has identical numbers, team to first send up persons with cards totaling number, wins point. For wrong answer deduct two points from score.

VARIATION: Award point to side sending up largest number of cards to total number.

Mock Track and Field Meet. Advance publicity helps build up enthusiasm for this occasion. If possible, divide into sides in advance and allow each group to elect captains. Give each team list of events and let them assign various players to specific events. However, don't tell true nature of event.

If group is extremely large, provide roles on each team for cheerleaders, bands, doctor and nurse, homecoming king and queen. Try to get everyone in the act. Encourage cheerleaders and team captains to keep enthusiasm high.

Two types of track meets are presented. One is for indoors, campfire, and rainy-day activity. Other is outdoor version incorporating more activity. Both will provide great fun for any group. As example, suggested number of participants from each team is presented for each event.

Indoor Events (may also be used outdoors):

50-Yard Dash: (Request fastest one on each team.) First to thread needle and take 50 stitches on piece of cloth, wins.

Javelin Throw: (Pair from each team.) Throw soda straws or feather for distance. Variation: Throw for accuracy at large bull's-eye drawn on floor.

Discus Throw: (Two players from each team.) Sail paper plate or powder puff as far as possible.

Hurdles: (One player from each team.) Peanuts in shell sprinkled along each course. Peanuts must be shelled and eaten as they are picked up.

Standing Broad Grin: (Two players from each team.) Measure grins and allow one winner. Prize is lemon or ripe persimmon.

Boarding House Reach: (One player from each team.) Measure armspread from fingertip to fingertip.

440 Yard Relay: (Two players from each team.) Push penny across yardstick with toothpick held in teeth. Run it relay fashion.

High Jump: (Two players from each team.) Contestants with hands tied behind backs jump for suspended doughnut. Tie doughnuts 6 inches over head of each participant.

Hammer Throw: (Two players from each team.) Inflate paper bag and tie with string 3 feet long. Contestants hold loose end of string, whirl bag around head, and throw.

Shot Put: (Two players from each team.) Contestants throw balloon or ball of cotton as far as possible. Variation: Contestant singing highest note wins.

Mile Relay: (Eight players from each team.) Each team has ball of twine. First man holds end of string and unwraps ball, passing it around himself once. He then passes it to next player and so on down line. Last man begins to rewind string and starts it back up line. First team to rewrap ball of twine, wins.

Low Jump: (Four players from each team.) Contestants pass under string without touching. Start at 3 feet and work down. Touching string disqualifies contestant. It is a surprise how low some can get!

Two-Mile Race: (One player with biggest feet from each team.) Contestants heel and toe around course. First one to complete the circuit, wins.

Tug of War: (One player from each team paired with one from another team.) String 3 feet long with marshmallow in the middle. Contestant holds one end in his mouth. First one to chew up string and reach marshmallow, wins. Don't swallow, of course.

Marathon Race: (All players from each team.) Give each one peanut. They then push peanut across room with their noses.

Refreshment Time: Everyone participates. Don't forget this event.

Outdoor Field Day (Use also indoor events ideas.) Relays and races suggested here incorporate much activity with minimum of skill. Boys and girls, when used in equal numbers on teams, can enjoy and participate in these activities together. Points can be awarded and running score kept for competing teams. Allow 5 points for first-place finish and three, two, and one for second, third, and fourth-place finishes. Since much enthusiasm is generated in these events, leader should limit number of events in which players enter in order that all will have equal participation. Playing area should be marked off in advance and loudspeaker secured if possible. Events suggested for this Field Day are described in active game section of this book.

Wheelbarrow Relay: (Equal number from each team.)

Sack Race: (Equal number from each team.)

Egg Throw for Distance: (Two players from each team.)

50-Yard Dash: (Any number.)

10-Yard Dash: (Any number.)

Dizzy Izzy Relay: (Equal number of players from each team.)

Centipede Race: (Equal number of players from each team, girls riding boys' backs.)

Backward Three-Legged Race: (Two players from each team.)

Medley Relay: (Eight players from each team.). Example: First player duckwalks 50 feet down course, tags next; second player crabwalks back; third player on hands and knees pushes ball with nose; fourth player puts ball between knees and returns to starting area; fifth and sixth players pick up seventh and carry her, chariot style, 25 yards down course; seventh player gets off and runs 75 yards down course; eighth player (anchor man) runs 100 yards back to finish line.

PHYSICAL FEATS AND STUNTS

These games and contests involve one or two persons. Some are tests of strength and agility. Others are merely stunts for laughs. All can be used effectively in campfire settings, as breathers between strenuous activity, or as a series of small group fun.

Egg-Throwing Contest (Age: 11 up)

EQUIPMENT: Eggs.
FORMATION: Players lined up in row, side by side, partners in similar row, facing them, three feet away.
DIRECTIONS: Players in first row are given one egg each. On signal, they throw eggs to their partners. Receivers take one step back and return egg to their partners. Throwing continues, each time one of partners stepping back, until championship is awarded to partner who can throw greatest distance without breaking egg. Best record we have heard of is 85 feet!

Apple Bobbing (Age: 8 up)

EQUIPMENT: Tub of water with apples floating in it.
FORMATION: Teams.
DIRECTIONS: Contestants kneel with hands behind back and try to bring apple out with their teeth.
VARIATION: Apple Biting.
DIRECTIONS: Apples tied with string to links or door casing or standards over head. Height of apple adjusted to contestant. Contestant should barely reach apple when on tiptoes. First one to get bite wins.

Indian Hand Wrestle (Age: 8 up)

FORMATION: Players stand with wide-legged stance, outside of right feet together, and grasping right hands. (This is reversed when done lefthanded.)
DIRECTIONS: On signal they jerk, pull, shove with right hand and wrist, trying to force opponent off balance. Object is to get opponent to move either foot. Left hand cannot be used, and cannot touch ground.

Pull-Up Contest (Age: 9 up)

FORMATION: Contestants sit on ground facing each other. Knees are straight, and feet are braced flat against opponents' feet.
DIRECTIONS: Each grasps strong stick between them (over toes) and tries to pull his opponent to him. If contestant bends his knees, he forfeits.

Blind Monkeys (Age: 10 up)

EQUIPMENT: Blindfold and bag of peanuts for each couple.

FORMATION: Couples.
DIRECTIONS: Couples are blindfolded and given peanuts. Man shells them and feeds them to his partner. Winner is group that eats most peanuts first.

Stone, Paper, Scissors (Age: 11 up)

FORMATION: Pairs, opponents facing one another.
DIRECTIONS: Leader counts "1, 2, 3," and on "3" the players bring hands forward from behind backs. Each player has his hands in position for stone, paper, or scissors. Stone is clenched fist, paper is open palm, scissors is a V formed by middle and index fingers. Stone beats scissors, paper beats stone, and scissors beat paper. Keep count of winnings and play until one person has won 5 times.
VARIATIONS: Play with two sides: have quarterback for each group who signals what sign will be used. On 3, both sides flash their sign.
Rabbit, Hunter, Gun or Fox, Hunter, Gun played in similar fashion. Rabbit sign made by placing a hand behind each ear to represent rabbit ears; gun sign made by aiming hands and fingers; hunter represented by standing with hands crossed over chest.

Hand Slap (Age: 11 up)

FORMATION: Pairs.
DIRECTIONS: One of couple has his hands extended palms down. Other person has palms up, underneath hands of first person.
OBJECT: Person underneath tries to slap hands of person on top by quickly withdrawing them and striking hands on top before they are withdrawn. If person on bottom fails, person on top gets to change and become hitter.

Hand Push (Age: 11 up)

FORMATION: Two players face each other arms length apart. Arms are extended, palm out.
DIRECTIONS: Players, on signal to begin, hit palms together, pushing, until one player loses his balance. Object is to make opponent move one or both feet. It is not permitted to strike body or arms. Only hands are hit.

Chinese Get-Up (Age: 6 up)

FORMATION: Two players sit back to back with arms folded.
DIRECTIONS: Each player tries to get up by pushing against other.
VARIATION: Try same contest with arms locked.

Indian Leg Wrestle (Age: 8 up)

FORMATION: Contestants lie side by side with feet in opposite directions. Adjacent arms are locked.
DIRECTIONS: On signal, adjacent legs are raised and locked at knee. Object is to force opponent over by bringing his knee back so that he must roll over.

Over the Toe Jump (Age: 12 up)

FORMATION: Stunt. Player stands on right foot and holds left toe by the right hand.

DIRECTIONS: Player springs off his right foot and tries to jump over the arch formed by his left leg and right arm. Several times are usually needed before balance is attained. Dropping toe by hand does not count in successful jump.

Stick Acrobatics (Age: 12 up)

FORMATION: Stunt. Player holds 3-foot stick behind his back with palms forward.

DIRECTIONS: Player brings stick over his head to position in front of his body without losing grip on stick. Lowers stick and steps over it from front with right foot. Continues, head first, raising left hand over head and passing stick over back. Now lifts left foot off floor and steps backward through stick. This can be repeated by starting backward and going backward through routine. Stick must always be held by both hands, but they can slide slightly to shorten or lengthen stick.

Cossack Dance (Age: 12 up)

FORMATION: Stunt. Player in deep knee bend or squat position with arms folded on chest.

DIRECTIONS: Player hops on his right foot and extends his left foot forward with heel touching floor. He hops on right foot again and brings left leg back to original position. This is repeated with other foot. After gaining proficiency, legs may be interchanged on a single hop. Also they may be extended sideways, or backward. Clapping hands or suitable music adds to performance of this stunt.

Knee Dip (Age: 10 up)

FORMATION: Player stands on foot and grasps other foot behind back with opposite hand.

DIRECTIONS: Squat on one leg and touch bent knee to ground, and stand up again. Do this in one movement.

One-Legged Knee Bend (Age: 10 up)

FORMATION: Player stands on one leg with other leg straight forward.

DIRECTIONS: Player goes down into a squatting position by bending supporting leg and comes up again and repeats with other leg.

Tip Up (Age: 10 up)

FORMATION: Player assumes squat position with hands on floor between knees.

DIRECTIONS: Player tilts body forward. Knees are pressed against elbows. Weight is on hands as feet come off floor. Player tries to maintain balanced position as long as possible without falling forward or allowing feet to touch floor.

Bulldog Pull (Age: 10 up)

FORMATION: Two players on all fours, facing each other, with heads close together. Belt, strap, or rope is looped around heads of both players.

DIRECTIONS: Each player tries to pull other forward a few feet. If either ducks his head and allows strap to be pulled off, he loses round. Two out of three trials determine winner.

Jump the Stick (Age: 12 up)

FORMATION: Stunt. Player holds stick in front of his body, with palms facing back.

DIRECTIONS: Player jumps up high, bends and tucks legs, at same time pulling stick under feet. This stunt can also be done by starting with stick in rear.

Tractor Pull (Age: 10 up)

FORMATION: Two larger persons are competing tractors; get on hands and knees and face opposite directions. Two smaller persons get atop tractors (one on each ''tractor''), facing in directions of their tractors.

DIRECTIONS: Holding on with his legs, each rider reaches both hands back to grip hands of his opponent. When pull is made, the rider who is unseated loses.

Toe Tilt (Age: 10 up)

FORMATION: Two players sit on floor or ground facing each other with knees bent, feet flat on ground, and arms clasped around their legs. Under knees and over arms of each is a wand or broomstick.

DIRECTIONS: At signal, each player tries to lift with his toes feet of his opponent. One who succeeds compels his opponent to lose his balance and roll over on his back.

Rooster Fight (Age: 9 up)

FORMATION: Two players stand in a circle drawn about 6 feet in diameter. Each puts his right hand behind his back, clasps his left foot with it, and then grips his right arm with his left hand behind his back.

DIRECTIONS: Players hop toward one another trying to force each other out of circle. If player lets go of foot or arm, or steps out of circle, he loses.

VARIATION: Players may fold arms over chests, grasp own elbows, instead of position above.

Chicken Fight (Age: 9 up)

FORMATION: Two players stand in circle drawn about 8 feet in diameter. They stoop and grasp their own ankles.

DIRECTIONS: Players try to push each other out of circle or off balance. Player who leaves circle, releases either hand, or touches ground with any part of his body other than his feet, loses contest.

Equipment and Skill Games

8

One of the best of group absorbers, equipment games should form an important part of the repertoire of most groups. Such games as ping-pong, shuffleboard, basketball goal shooting are fairly common. A few ball games are familiar. Here are some games which can be assembled easily, many of them made of scrap or waste materials, and nearly all from very inexpensive materials.

These games perform a fine function in occupying people as they first arrive. Pick out ten or fifteen of them, have them around the walls. (Sometimes they are used as special features in carnivals staged by clubs, schools, or churches.)

Simple skill games make wonderful family night activities, whether rolling, tossing, sliding or bouncing kinds. Families might be encouraged to make some of these games.

Picnics are naturals for equipment games, if that kind of fun is needed. Notice how easily some of the tossing games could be rigged up. (Of course, the old standby, horseshoes or quoits, may be added.) Washer tossing is inexpensive and satisfying. A rainy day at camp calls for bringing out a number of skill games, such as these, to see who can do it best. Set players to planning new games.

TOSSING GAMES

Probably the most popular games in the simple skill category are those that involve tossing at, into, or through something. Work up your own game and make your own rules! Here are some of the most popular articles to toss:

1. Bean bags
2. Balls, marbles
3. Quoits (fruit jar rubbers, rope rings, quoits made of hose, even cardboard hoops or barrel hoops)
4. Rubber heels
5. Discs like checkers, linoleum discs, metal washers, curtain rings
6. Feathers, darts
7. Even stones, seeds, fruit, or vegetables
8. Horseshoes, shoes
9. Clothespins (usually dropped)
10. Things difficult to toss any distance, like feathers, toothpicks, soda straws, balls of cotton, cords, cards, paper plates, envelopes

These objects are tossed *into* the following receptacles:

1. Tin cans of various sizes
2. Cake pans
3. Wide-mouthed bottles
4. Egg cartons (with sections numbered for points)

5. Cups
6. Barrels
7. Holes in ground
8. Holes in bean bag board, or side of box, usually numbered for points, smaller, harder holes bearing higher points
9. Basketball goal

They are also tossed *onto*—

1. Targets like archery target, targets on floor
2. Squares, each having different value depending on how hard it is to hit

They are tossed *at*—

1. Archerylike targets (for darts)
2. Special boards having special value, like dart baseball

In tossing games, you may make your own rules of the game, your own combination of objects to be tossed, what they're to be tossed *into* or *onto*.

Washer Tossing. Like horseshoes, in many ways. Holes in ground (or tin cans) are 10 to 20 feet apart (depending on ability of players). Some count washers in hole three points; some five. Usually game is played to 21. Washer on washer in hole cancels. Closest washer of same color (washers have been painted) count one each. It is customary to pitch from two to four washers, alternating in turn. Small tin cans nailed onto wide boards are used for washer tossing indoors. Some craftsmen are skillful enough to set cans *into* boards, flush with edge of board so that washers can slide in! Make your own rules, your own points, your own distances. Here is an opportunity to create something of your own!

Games with Fruit Jar Rubbers

1. Drive nails in board and number value of each nail. Give each person five fruit jar rubbers to toss from distance of 6 to 10 feet.
2. Dodo is a version of this. One nail or hook is called Dodo and counts off. All others are valued as numbered. Play to total score of 50 or whatever is agreed upon in advance.
3. Use fingers upon which to toss rubbers. Two partners, standing six feet apart, are competing with another couple in same fashion. Each person tosses five rubbers to his partner's fingers, and counts one point for each successful try. Then partner tosses the five back. Game may be played to see who gets 25 or 50 points first, or who has best score in specified number of total tosses (between team members) like 30, 50.
4. Spring clothespins are fastened on side of box or bucket, with value of each pin written on it. Players toss fruit jar rubbers to try to ring clothespins.
5. Played in partners, one person holds up clothespin, and other tries to toss fruit jar rubbers onto clothespin, with partner helping. Score as in No. 3.
6. Turn chair upside down and toss fruit jar rubbers at legs from 6 to 10 feet back. One point for each successful toss.
7. Several soft-drink bottles are lined up. Object: to toss fruit jar rubbers onto necks of bottles from 6 to 10 feet back.

Quoit Tossing (any kind of hoops, rope rings)

1. Turn chair upside down and toss rope rings at legs, points counted for successful tries, such as 10. Cardboard rings cut from oatmeal boxes will do.
2. Toss quoits over soft-drink bottle or milk bottles, count points for successes.
3. Put clothespins on cardboard box. Count points for successful ringers.
4. Quoit golf. Make nine pegs by sawing off lengths of broom handles and nailing them onto boards as bases. Set these out as if on golf course and count against each player number of tosses necessary to make rounds. (No toss can be made from less than 3 feet away.)

Tossing Larger Balls. Games have been devised for tossing volleyballs, basketballs, footballs. softballs, such as these:

1. Baseball throw into barrel, or through barrel hoop.
2. Football throw for accuracy, distance. (Same with other balls.)
3. Bouncing volleyball, basketball into can, wastebasket, barrel.
4. Basketball free throws—see who gets most out of 10 tries.
5. Toss or throw any of these balls for certain line or spot, such as nearest to base.

Tossing Paper Plates

1. Toss or sail for distance. See who can toss farthest.
2. Toss or sail plates through barrel hoop or wire ring, suspended from ceiling, door. Count points for each successful try.
3. Toss or sail through Christmas wreath, large heart, turkey outline made of wire, pumpkin outline made of wire or other seasonal device.
4. Toss or sail paper plates into wastebasket, or through basketball goal.

Tossing Checkers, Corks, Pebbles, Marbles, Curtain Rings, Milk Bottle or Coke Caps, Small Wooden Cubes

1. Toss specified number (5 to 10) into small end of megaphone.
2. Toss into a No. 10 can from 10 to 15 feet back.
3. Toss into flower pots, each one marked for score, from 8 to 15 feet back.
4. Toss into muffin tins, with each hole numbered for points. (In case of cube, count points for marking on each side: 5, 10, 15, 20, 25, 30—or 1 to 6).
5. Toss into a cake pan with center hole, scoring five points for hitting pan, 25 points if hit hole, from 8 to 10 feet back.
6. Tossing into egg carton, with each hole numbered for points, like 2, 3, 5. Count total score after tossing 25 times, or devise your own system.
7. Make cardboard diagram one foot square or larger, with the mystic 15 on it. Each player gets points in keeping with where their marker stops. (Marbles are not suitable for this.) If anyone gets exactly 15, it doubles score.
8. Suspend horseshoe 6 to 8 feet away from line and let contestants try to toss through horseshoe.
9. Suspend 8-inch hoop from door or ceiling and then within the hoop suspend bell. Object: From distance of 6 to 8 feet, to toss an object through hoop

without ringing bell. For each success, 5 to 10 points. (A ping-pong ball is good for this.)

10. Throw rocks at fence posts. Point for each hit.
11. From 20 feet back, toss objects into barrel, counting points for each success.
12. Toss into box through holes in side. Place number value on each hole. Play for highest score in 10 tosses, or to specified score, such as 50.
13. Draw diagram as indicated. Toss flat discs (checkers, milk bottle caps, coke caps). Bull's-eye doubles, triangle halves score, corner diamonds cancel score, up to point it was hit. Take 10 trials.

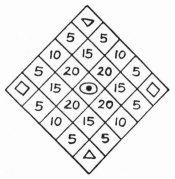

14. Toss into cans of different sizes, one set inside the other, with highest points for hitting smallest cans.
15. Make hoops of different sizes from wire or wood strips and place point value on each one. Toss objects into hoops, counting points as indicated. Stand 6 to 12 feet away.

Match Darts. Make three darts by cutting heads from matches, slitting one end so that piece of folded paper about 2½ inches square can be slipped in. Force large sewing needle into other end. (Feather might be substituted for paper.) Target as shown is 15 to 18 inches in diameter on outside.

Players stand 8 feet away, and each tries to hit bull's-eye, counting whatever score he makes.

Piercing the Hoop. Suspend barrel hoop from tree and let players throw fishing pole or its equivalent through hoop. Each one gets three to five tries. Start from about 15 feet back, gradually go farther back to encourage more skill.

Ring the Hook. Screw good-sized hook into a wall or pole. Put curtain ring or harness ring on one end of string and tie other end to branch of tree or suspend from ceiling, testing length of hook to make sure ring can catch there easily. Object: to stand back, swing ring up and catch it on hook. Many camps have several of them in trees or on sides of buildings for informal play. (This game has amazing drawing power!)

Roman Star Toss. Points are counted in Roman numerals. Bean bags, rubber heels, washers or other tossing items may be used. Line is about 6 feet away from diagram which has been chalked or marked on floor or on paper. All divisions must be somewhat larger than whatever is tossed. Anything touching line does not count. Each player tosses in rotation. Predetermine total points to win, but make rule that no player may win with first toss. (That is, if 500 is winning score, player may not win by tossing D or an M.)

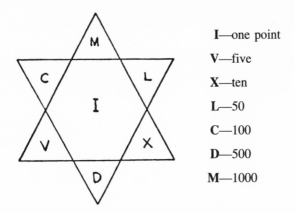

I—one point

V—five

X—ten

L—50

C—100

D—500

M—1000

How to Make Bean Bag Boards. These may be simple or more complex. Here is one example.

Make board 2 feet wide, 2½ to 3 feet long. Cut holes as illustrated. Eyes are 7 × 5 inches, mouth is 10 × 4 inches, base of triangle 8 inches. Place board against building or give it hinged prop.

Players stand 10 to 15 feet back of board. Each has 5 bean bags (or other specified number). See who gets most in five pitches, or play to certain score, such as 100. May be played on team basis, each person pitching one bag.

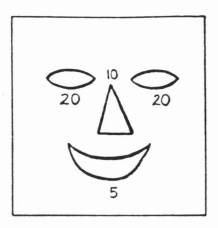

Games with Bean Bags or Rubber Heels

KITCHEN GOLF. With kitchen utensils placed in zigzag fashion around room or outdoor space, play in couples or by individuals. Each has bean bags to toss into these utensils, keeping score. As soon as one couple has finished with first hole, another starts.

TARGET GAME. Toss bean bags at target on floor, each player getting specified number of tosses, such as three, in rotation. Play to specified score to win like 25, 50, or 100.

500. Players are in sixes, each having bean bag. Target is made with center circle of 1 foot, next circle 1½ feet, next one 2½ feet, outside one 3½ feet, and all is enclosed in 7-foot square. Players toss from line 10 to 20 feet back (depending on skill and age). Object: to be first to make perfect score of exactly 500 with six bean bags.

Rules: Bean bags resting on line are tossed again, those making score are left in place. Captain of either team has privilege of returning any bean bag not making sufficient score. At end, an exact score of 500 must be recorded to win.

BEAN BAG TOSS. Using target similar to No. 3, have players toss and keep individual scores. See who gets highest total in five tosses, ten tosses.

BEAN BAG SHUFFLEBOARD. With bean bags or rubber heels, toss or slide on shuffleboard court, counting as in shuffleboard.

Bean Bag Golf

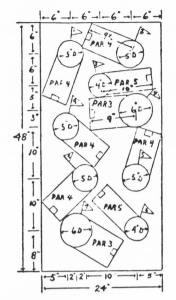
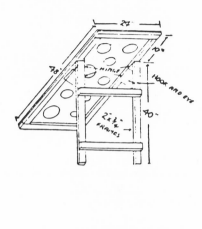

OBJECT: Using bean bags, to get around nine-hole golf course in fewest number of throws or strokes. Par for course is 36. You cannot toss more than par for any hole. If you have not holed out, you take par for your score for that hole. Entire group playing move from hole to hole, as in golf.

Bean Bag Basketball. Five players are on team, each one shooting from goal line edge of diagram (chalked on floor or otherwise marked). First player tosses bean bag and gets what diagram indicates. If he hits "Side shoots again," next player in line takes over toss and he goes to foot of his line. If he makes goal he keeps shooting. When player has finished his turn he goes to foot of his line, and other side takes over. If bean bag lands midway on line, player shoots again; otherwise it counts for side on which most of bag lies. On free shots, player gets free tosses, then shoots again. Only thing on diagram that counts in "free shots" is a goal, which counts one point for each success. (Regular goal is 2 points.)

Play for specified length of time, such as 5-minute quarters. More players than five on team can be used. Also in large room, several games could be going at same time.

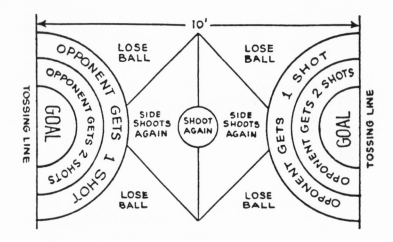

Bean Bag Baseball. Play with two teams. Each batter continues to toss bean bags until out or on base. Regular baseball rules apply.

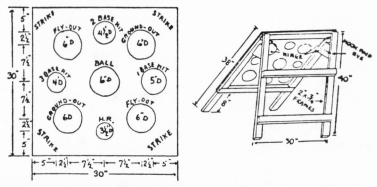

Baseball Tossing Game. Mark this diagram on floor:

HOME RUN	TRIPLE	DOUBLE	WALK
FLY OUT	STRIKE OUT	FOUL OUT	3 BAGGER
WALK	DOUBLE	WALK	HOME RUN
SINGLE	OUT	DOUBLE	OUT

Toss onto diagram metal washers, rubber heels, or bean bags. Two teams play. Each player tosses, in turn, until on base or out. Rules are as in baseball.

Dart Baseball. There are two teams. Batting team tosses darts, first player until he gets on base or out. Same rules as baseball, with teams changing sides after three outs. Play as many innings as are desirable. Darts can be bought at sporting goods stores.

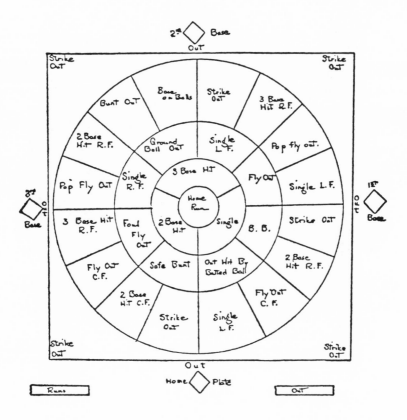

Seasonal Tossing Games. Using rubber heels, bean bags, or other things to toss, draw diagram on floor in keeping with season, such as the following:

THANKSGIVING (draw outline of turkey): breast, score of 20; leg, 10; wing, 5; neck, 5.

HALLOWE'EN (draw jack-o-lantern): nose, 20; eyes, 15 each; mouth, 10; ears, 5 each.

CHRISTMAS: small star in center, with larger ones surrounding. Largest score in center.

ROLLING GAMES

There are innumerable miniature games that can be played with golf, ping-pong, and small rubber balls, or with marbles. Some are in imitation of standard games such as golf, dodge ball, hockey, polo.

Clock Golf. Played in circle, 15 to 40 feet in diameter, with positions numbered, 1 to 12, around circumference like clock face. Hole into which to putt is placed anywhere in circle. It is wide and deep enough for ball used.

Golf or hockey sticks or even knotted tree branches are used to putt ball, which may be golf ball or rubber ball about that size. Each player plays around clock, trying to do it in smallest number of strokes.

Obstacle Golf. This small-space game uses tin cans, bent tin tunnels, mounds, trenches, soil pipe. Holes are laid out as in regular golf, with tin cans 4 inches in diameter sunk in ground (holes in bottom to let water through in case of rain). Instead of smooth course these obstacles are deliberately planned. Object is to get around course in fewest strokes.

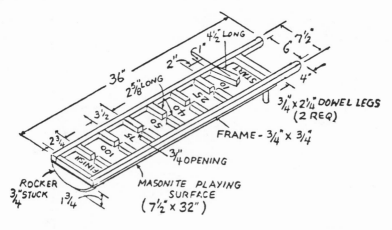

Marble Dodging Game. Object is to get as many as possible in high-point stalls before one sneaks through to finish. Ten marbles are used. Game is played by placing all marbles in section marked start. Player takes track by handles, raises it slightly, turns it back and forth on rocker to get marbles to roll through narrow openings into spaces with progressively higher point value.

When marble slips through to finish line, place game down on its legs immediately and tally score. Then next player takes his turn.

Table Polo

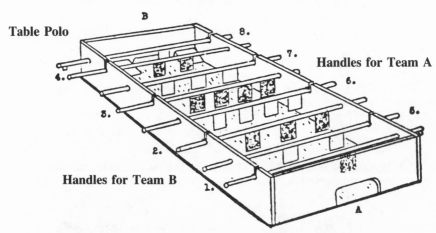

Handles for Team A

Handles for Team B

DIRECTIONS FOR CONSTRUCTING: Using ¾-inch thick limber, cut out sides and ends of box as per diagram. Note slots cut in sides, only *four* to side. These slots should be slightly wider than thickness of paddle material so as to facilitate removal of paddle assemblies by turning paddles upward and sliding out. Note that sides of box are cut in ⅜ inch at ends to make stronger joint. This way, screws can be used on both sides of each corner. By having bottom of holes on sides $3\frac{1}{8}$ inches from box floor and with paddles 3 inches long, there would be clearance of $\frac{1}{8}$ inch between bottom of paddles and box floor.

From Masonite cut piece $21\frac{1}{2}$ inches $\times$ 48 inches and using smooth side for playing surface, nail it on bottom of box frame. From pieces of scrap wood make four incline boards and fasten these in each corner.

Using discarded mop or broom handles and Masonite scrap, make eight paddle assemblies—two of each of four shown. Sheet metal $\frac{1}{32}$ inch thick may be used instead of Masonite. Note that paddle goes all way up through handle and is fastened with glue and small bolts.

Stops are necessary on two paddle assemblies with only one paddle because their movement is restricted by corner incline boards. "Stops" are optional on other paddle assemblies, but if used, should be fastened to handles so that paddles just miss touching side walls. Stops can easily be removed to facilitate removal of paddle assemblies from box.

Thoroughly sand game box and equipment before either varnishing, staining, or painting.

DIRECTIONS FOR PLAYING: There are two teams with 2 to 4 players on each team. One team stand on one side of box and play paddle assemblies 1, 2, 3, 4. They have as their goal end B. Second team stand on opposite side and play paddle assemblies 5, 6, 7, 8, and have end A as their goal. Goal for any team is always to players' left. A ping-pong ball is used and paddles are players. Game starts with ball thrown into middle of box between paddle assemblies with four paddles.

Object of game is for each team to get ball through their goal, at same time preventing their opponents from doing same thing and scoring. Each ball going through opening at either end scores one point. Any arbitrary number of points decided upon by teams can constitute game. If ball is hit out of box, it is tossed into center of box, and play is resumed.

To make game faster when from 4 to 8 people are playing, two balls are used at same time. However, team must get *both* balls through their goal before point is scored. If both teams get one ball each, no point is scored.

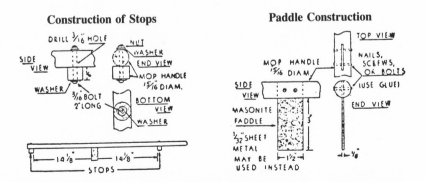

Construction of Stops   **Paddle Construction**

Basket Hockey. Two to four persons can play with this board on table. Using hockey sticks they attempt to drive marble through their opponent's goal, up and around and into basket. Marble is put into play by dropping in center of playing field.

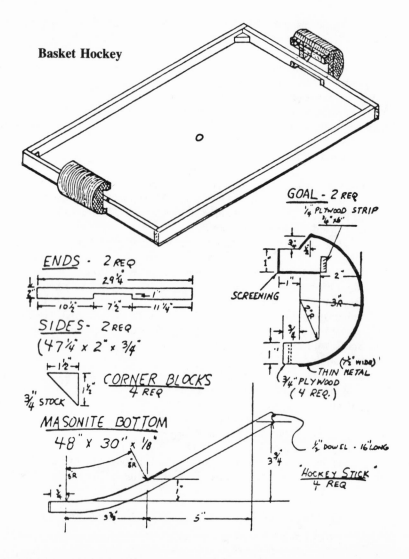

Basket Hockey

GOAL - 2 REQ

ENDS · 2 REQ

SIDES - 2 REQ
($47\frac{1}{4}" \times 2" \times \frac{3}{4}"$)

CORNER BLOCKS
4 REQ
$\frac{3}{4}"$ STOCK

MASONITE BOTTOM
$48" \times 30" \times \frac{1}{8}"$

$\frac{1}{2}"$ DOWEL · 16" LONG

HOCKEY STICK
4 REQ

CONSTRUCTION: Build frame with ends and side pieces; note overlapping joints. Attach Masonite bottom, smooth side up, to frame and add corner blocks.

Goals are constructed by tacking thin sheet of tin to two $\frac{3}{4}$-inch plywood sides shown. Insert $\frac{1}{4}$-inch plywood strip and nail. Wire screening is fastened to front to form basket. Basket goals can then be inserted into openings at each end until metal is flush with Masonite bottom. Holes can be drilled through frame at each prong of goals, and nails used to hold the goals more firmly to frame.

Hockey sticks are $\frac{1}{2}$-inch dowels steamed and bent into shape. Make form for bending sticks before steaming, and then after steaming let stick remain on form until dry. A five-quart oil can with approximately 1-inch diameter hole in top will serve for steaming. Add ½ inch of water to can and heat on stove to boiling; place stick in can and let steam for 10 minutes or more.

Rolling Games with Simpler Equipment

1. Little children like to roll a ball back and forth with other children or adults, sitting on floor.
2. Rolling ball into can or series of cans, counting points for successful tries is fun for children and older folk. (Balls from small golf size to large size, with cans in proportion.)
3. Set three milk bottles up with few inches between them. Try to roll ball or marbles between bottles without clinking. Points for successful tries.
4. Cut holes larger than marbles in side of cigar box and turn box upside down, as shown. Each player shoots or rolls marbles into holes from appropriate distance away.

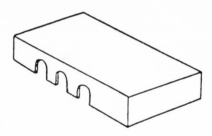

5. Roll small ball up flap of egg carton, into carton. Points counted for successful tries, with different squares having different point values.
6. MINIATURE BOWLING. Buy set of small tenpins at specialty store and use small rubber balls to knock them down by rolling, scoring as in regular bowling. (Another version is to suspend ball on string in doorway, set up pins there, pull ball back and let it swing on string, knocking down pins.)
7. Cardboard milk cartons are good tenpins, if ball large enough to knock them over is used. (Also blocks of wood or tenpins, tin cans.)
8. Marble bowling is accomplished by using large nails or spikes, sitting on their heads, as tenpins, and scoring as in regular tenpins.
9. GOLF. Try putting into cans set up at end of room. See how many times you can hit can in five tries, or make own rules.
10. GOOFY GOLF. Lay out course outdoors, use hockey sticks and small rubber ball, play as in regular golf.
11. CORK GOLF. Shape coat hanger into putter and use cork. Hole is chalked or otherwise marked at other end of room. See who can "hole out" in fewest strokes.
12. AUTOMOBILE RACE. Lay out course on floor or table, marking numbered areas within last 12 inches. Push toy autos down speedway into scoring area. Object may be (1) to get them to stop closest to finish line, or (2) to get cars to race across finish line first.

13. TABLE LEAF BOWLING. Use a 3½- to 4-foot table leaf for alley. To bottom side of table leaf screw piece of ¼ inch plywood which is about 6 inches wider than leaf so that leaf is centered on plywood, and that plywood extends 5 inches beyond one end of leaf.

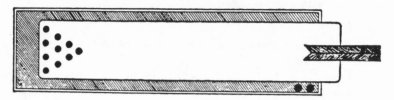

Around edge of plywood screw strips of wood ¾ inch thick and 2 inches high to form gutters. Next, screw together two pieces of ¼-inch plywood about 12 inches long and 2 inches wide to form V-shaped trough down which to roll balls. This trough should be cut at slant at one end so that it will rest on alley at a 45° angle. Finally, paint spots at other end of alley to represent position of pins. Use wooden pins bought from toy or "dime-store," and three wooden balls. Score as in tenpins.

DROPPING, BOUNCING, AND PUSHING GAMES

Besides the scores of tossing and rolling games that require simple equipment there are many games in which a ball or a disc is dropped or bounced into a container, or pushed around a charted area.

Dropping Clothespins, Nuts, Pebbles, Coins

1. Dropping clothespins into milk bottles from back of chair, counting points for number out of five pins dropped that go in.
2. Same, but each pin has value marked on its head. Score points by checking heads of successful pins. Head of certain color, such as red, might double score.
3. Drop pin, one from each shoulder, from nose, and from each eye, bending over milk bottle. Count points for successful tries.
4. Same idea as above, but using nuts or coins.
5. Drop five coins into fishbowl half-filled with water, containing small glass. Count one point for each coin going into bowl, five points for those going into glass.

Bouncing Games

1. Bounce ball from distance of 6 to 10 feet, into wastebasket or box of similar size. Count points for each success. Try two bounces and in!
2. Bounce ball (up to tennis ball size) on floor, off wall, and catch it in funnel.
3. Bounce ball over back of chair and into wastebasket or box, or bucket.
4. Bounce ping-pong ball on table and into egg carton.
5. Cut 6-inch holes in large piece of canvas and mount it perpendicular to ground. Players bounce tennis ball (or other small ball) on ground and through holes, each of which is marked for points (5, 10, 15, 25, and so on).

Maze. Maze is home-made skill game, incorporating shooting of caroms with three-foot long ⅜-inch dowel rod, and it can be played by 2 to 8 persons. (Carom here is a wooden disc flipped with finger.)

Board is 3 × 4 feet with ½-inch square molding (glued and nailed securely) around edge and along all heavy lines. (See diagram.) Hazards are painted in red. Advantages are painted in green.

MAZE

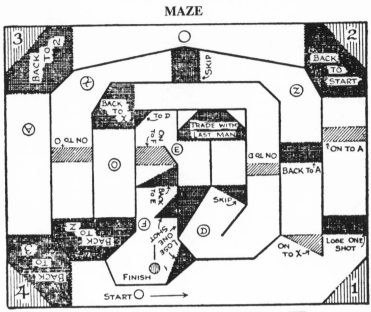

Color Code: Blue ▤ Green ▨ Red ▥

Object of game is to shoot your caroms into each corner pocket (1, 2, 3, and 4) and then continue shooting through maze area until carom is upon blue-finish circle. First player to do so is winner.

Additional materials needed: a different colored or marked carom for each participant. Cues (⅜-inch dowel rod) for each player or every other player. (If there are not enough cues to go around, players can trade back and forth, since they play in turn.)

Rules:

1. Determine by lot shooting order (take turns).
2. First shot is from Start Circle toward corner pocket 1. (Each time corner pocket is scored, shooter immediately gets another shot from pocket opening toward next objective.)
3. Carom must be completely on a color. (Color shows all way around before directions of markings can be followed.)
4. A player may not shoot backward to earn advance or to interfere with opponent. He may shoot back to try to make corner pocket.
5. As soon as carom stops on green advance, carom is moved to designated area.
6. If carom stops on red hazard, it remains until its next turn. Then it is played from its designated area.

7. A carom that jumps over partition is returned to spot from which it was shot; and next player continues.
8. If a carom rests too near partition for good shooting, it may be moved out to width of cue.
9. Opponents'caroms are not to be removed from board to facilitate shooting. They too become hazards, to be shot around or hit.
10. "Trade with Last Man" means to trade positions with person farthest from finish circle.

HINTS: Before difficult hazards, Back to Start, Back to Z, Back to 3, Back to X, and Trade with Last Man, it is often wise to shoot for advances and play cautiously. In rest of maze, play with boldness. Study angles of partitions and plan how to carom. It is often better to "lose one shot" than "trade with last man."

Regulation Shuffleboard. Diagram is painted or drawn on floor (It can be set in asphalt tile.) Regulation disc is 6 inches in diameter, 1 inch thick. Pusher (shovel) is about 5 feet long.

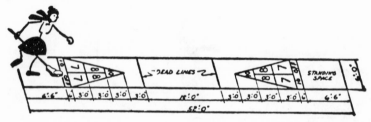

If two players play, each takes turns pushing his discs from standing space. (Discs are of two different colors for easy scoring.) No disc on lines counts. Game is to 50 points. If doubles are played, one partner is at each end of court. In all cases, player with larger score pushes first.

Deck Shuffleboard. This type is for smaller spaces. Diagram can be chalked on floor. (One leader carries a 1- × 3-foot piece of plywood, and a rounded-end 1- × 3-foot piece, and quickly marks diagram and numerals on floor.) Broomsticks can be used for pusher handles, and discs are usually smaller than regulation.

10
2	9	4
7	5	3
6	1	8
10 OFF		

Draw line 10 to 12 feet back from diagram. Play from 10 plus side.

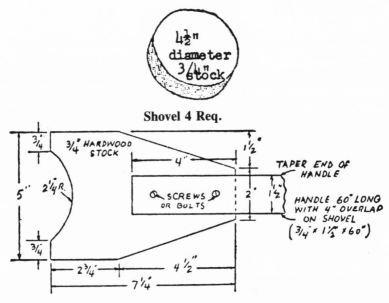

Shovel 4 Req.

Road Block. For two players, each holding twenty-six squares, 2″ × 2″, of colored cardboard, red for one player, yellow for the other. Note how the squares are marked, and that a different number of each of the five types of squares is marked as indicated, each player having 8 "corners," 11 "through roads," and so on.

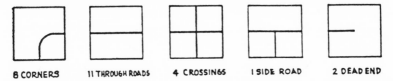

One player leads off. They play alternately. The object is to get 10 squares in a forward direction to win. (Side moves or backward moves do not count on the total of 10.) A player may, in turn, either play on his own "highway system" (offense) or on his opponent's to block him (defense). The latter may be done by placing a dead-end block to stop opponent's forward progress. Opponent must then start at a crossing or back behind the beginning, going in the other direction (which will now be considered "forward" for him). If in doubt, agree on your own rules.

Corner blocks may be used to turn opponent's line of progress into stopping place, as shown:

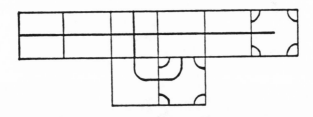

Marble Trap. This game can be played by two, three, or four, persons. Object of game is to "trap" opponents' marbles. Each has six marbles of a color.

Play: In turn, place one marble at a time on board, with hope of being able to have row of three of your color, while preventing others from doing same.

When any player succeeds in placing three marbles, of his color, in a straight row he has succeeded in making a "trap" and thereby is privileged to take one marble from each of his opponents, except from closed trap.

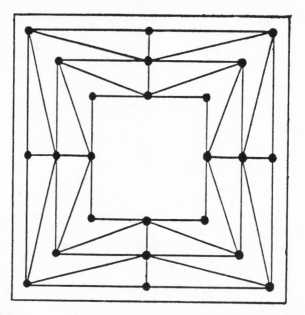

After all marbles have been placed on board they may be moved from one hole to next only in straight lines.

When player has but three marbles left he is privileged to "jump" his marble to any place on board (he does not have to follow lines as others do).

Persons having less than three marbles cannot make a "trap," so they are out of game. "Traps" may be opened and closed at will, providing opponent does not place his marble in strategic position.

Boards may be almost any size. Lines can be burned in with an iron.

Racing Game. Get piece of brown wrapping paper, 3 × 7 feet. With crayon, mark out race track similar to sketch. Track should be wide enough for three or four toy cars to stand side by side.

Mark numbers, 1 to 6, on sides of a block or cube. Let each player, in turn, roll block to see how many spaces to move his car. If he stops on space with written directions, he must follow these directions. Driver of car with bumper touching finish line first, wins. Continue to see who comes in for other positions.

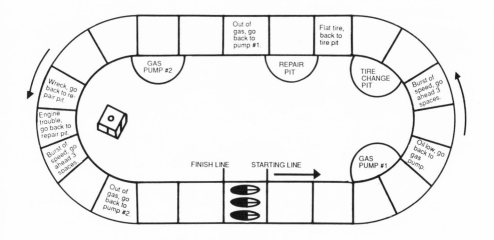

Battleship

PLAYERS: Two persons or group. Each group has form similar to one above.

Each player or side locates his ships on receiving board—1 Battleship (four squares), 1 Cruiser (three squares), 2 Destroyers (2 squares each), 4 Mines (one square each). Player is not allowed to see location of opponent's ships. Ships are located by circling proper number of squares in pencil. Ships may be located horizontally, vertically or diagonally.

Each player—playing in rotation—fires volley of seven shots at his opponent's ships. Volley consists of calling out to opponent, say, "B-7"; opponent marks this on his chart. Next might be "J-2," and so on. Shooter also keeps record on his chart, showing spots he shot on round 1 by placing figure 1 in all spots toward which he shoots. This consists simply of calling out numbers of spots where he thinks his opponent's equipment is located. These shots he records on sending board while his opponent records on receiving board. He must call letter and number of each square at which he fires.

Number 1 player places his seven shots and then asks his opponent, "Did I hit anything?" Player Number 2 must answer truthfully, but he does not tell where hit scored. He simply says, "Yes, you hit my battleship once. Nothing else." Then number 2 player shoots in same manner.

When a ship goes down, that player loses that many shots at his opponent ships—3 for Battleship, 2 for Cruiser, and 1 each for Destroyers. When mine is hit, firing player loses any remaining shots in that particular salvo. Player is not defeated until all his ships are sunk.

	1	2	3	4	5	6	7	8	9	10	11
A											
B											
C											
D											
E											
F											
G											
H											
I											
J											
K											

RECEIVING BOARD

	1	2	3	4	5	6	7	8	9	10	11
A											
B											
C											
D											
E											
F											
G											
H											
I											
J											
K											

SENDING BOARD

BATTLESHIP

CRUISER

DESTROYER

MINES

Outdoor Tetherball. Pole 10 feet high has rope or strong cord ($7\frac{1}{2}$ feet long) fastened at top, and ball of tennis-ball size or larger on other end of rope or cord. Line is marked on pole 6 feet high. Two play. Object: to wind ball around pole, make it touch above line.

Table Tether Ball (for two players)

CONSTRUCTION: Bore hole through center of board to fit mop handle. Attach two brackets with bolts to board. Insert handle and bolt. Attach screw eye to top of handle. Tie string to eye with ball on other end.

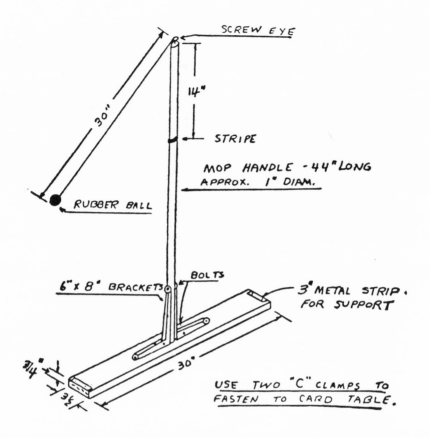

Rules: Each person uses a paddle. Ball is put in play by one player serving; he hits it with the idea of winding the string around the pole above stripe. Server may choose direction in which he desires to wind string. Opponent tries to hit ball back and wind it in opposite direction. Player fouls when he winds string around his paddle. Penalty for foul is free hit by opponent. If he can wind string around pole above stripe in one unimpeded stroke, he scores point. Players set score; anywhere from 5 to 15 points make game.

INDEX

158

02000050